BORROWER'S GUIDE TO COMMERCIAL LENDING

Small Business Lending
Commercial Realty
Asset based Lending
Equipment Financing
SBA Lending
More...

Richard W. Carrell

Evergreen House Publishing

Copyright 2014 Evergreen House Publishing LLC

All rights reserved by Evergreen House Publishing LLC. No part of this book may be reproduced in any manner or form, nor electronically stored, mechanically stored, in part or parts. The book cannot be copied, scanned for transfer. No part of this book can be quoted or used without permission of the owner.

Published by Evergreen House Publishing LLC
Medford, New Jersey 08055

This publication is designed to provide opinion and authoritative information in the areas in the book but is not designed to give any legal opinion, legal advice or any legal assistance or any other professional service other than commercial and business lending.

Print ISBN 13: 978-1-62217-146-0

Library of Congress

DEDICATION

One of joys of writing a book is the dedication. This book I dedicate to vast group of commercial borrowers who despite having a worthy deal were never able to obtain financing of a worthy project. It is very difficult to work with folks who have not been able to realize their dream. I have been lucky in not having to face that dilemma many times. One reason I always recommend commercial borrowers seek out expert help is make sure the borrowers get the best possible outcomes.

ABOUT THE AUTHOR

Richard W. Carrell has been associated with commercial lending for over 30 years. Educated at Washington College in Chestertown, Maryland, Mt. Vernon School of Law and the University Of Baltimore School Of Law, Mr. Carrell practiced law for over 25 years. In 1996, he began the natural transition to commercial and business lending. He became associated with Allegheny Financial LLC as counsel and manager of commercial lending. Mr. Carrell has been an officer of Allied Financial, Inc. serving as vice-present and general counsel. Presently, Mr. Carrell is the Executive Vice-President of Evergreen Commercial Finance Solutions, LLC. In addition, Mr. Carrell is Editor of Evergreen House Publishing Company LLC. From his experiences, he is continuing to write about the process of commercial real estate lending and business transactions.

In addition, a broker's addition of this present work will be released. This book will be called *Broker's Guide to Commercial Lending*. I hope that this book will assist people who are interested in the profession of commercial lending. This book should be available later this year.

Mr. Carrell has four grown children and is married to Brenda Carrell, president of Evergreen Commercial Finance Solutions, LLC. They reside in Medford, New Jersey with their two longhaired Shih Tzu's, Mattee and Samee. He is the author of *The Mindwrks Project*, using a nom de plume Richard Wayne.

SPECIAL NOTE FROM THE AUTHOR

At the time this book is being finished, the United States and the entire world are trying to dig out from the worst economic downturn in over 60 years. I was not alive to experience the Great Depression, but do remember the 70's and early 80's with double digit interest rates for residential loans and very difficult lending rules and high interest for commercial loans.

Obviously one of the key factors in restoring economic stability is the injection of capital into the system. One of the key ways is the use of commercial lending.

Now, as I look at the world of commercial lending, I see a return to "old fashion" conservative lending where banks are difficult to deal with and lending is very tight in order to deal with the difficult economic times. I see commercial lenders becoming more conservative. As a rule, a bank will take a pass on some loans many of which may have found a home in the past ten years. The lending bar has been raised to the point that the average commercial borrower will not be able to get the capital they need to move their business along without expert help. No longer can an average commercial borrower expect to just walk into a bank and sit down with a loan officer, work out a loan and close it without going through a nail biting, soul searching and exhaustive lending process.

Now, in order to cope with the *"new"* order of lending you must be better prepared to deal with the commercial lending process and the tight lending rules. Knowing as much as possible about the process can help. Hopefully, with increased awareness, you can put a better face on your loan as well as being able to explain your business and loan request. As you will learn, many good loans do not get done because of the manner in which the borrower presents the loan. With an increased understanding of the commercial loan process, your loan package along with your knowledge of the system will lead you to success.

Now more than ever it is vital to be better prepared to deal with commercial lenders. While I haven't a clue as to what the future of lending will hold, I do know that if you know as much as possible about the basics of lending you will be better prepared to deal with the process. It is my intention to give you a book that can help you succeed.

The four elements of a "loan" are, a principal sum, a placing of the sum with a safe borrower, an agreement that interest is to be paid, and recognition by receiver of money of liability to return of the principal amount with accrued Interest.

Black's Law Dictionary

TABLE OF CONTENTS

ABOUT THE AUTHOR — iv

SPECIAL NOTE FROM THE AUTHOR — v

INTRODUCTION — xiii

PART ONE: THE BORROWER — 1
CHAPTER 1. *What is a Small Business?* — 3
CHAPTER 2. *Options for Raising Capital* — 5

PART TWO: WHERE TO BEGIN — 15
CHAPTER 3. *Inventory of Your Finances* — 17
CHAPTER 4. *Determine Your Lending Needs* — 23
CHAPTER 5. *What Kind of Loan Do I need?* — 27
CHAPTER 6. *The Business Plan* — 37
CHAPTER 7. *Preparing the Loan Package* — 43
CHAPTER 8. *Submitting the Loan and Interview* — 51

PART THREE: THE LENDERS — 53
CHAPTER 9. *The Mysteries of Banking* — 55
CHAPTER 10. *Conventional Banks* — 57
CHAPTER 11. *What Makes a Borrower Eligible for a Bank Loan?* — 59
CHAPTER 12. *Economic Development Loans* — 67
CHAPTER 13. *Private Lenders* — 71
CHAPTER 14. *Seller Financing* — 75
CHAPTER 15. *Interest Rates and Fees* — 81

CHAPTER 16. *Private Lenders' Rates* 85

PART FOUR: THE LOAN PROCESS 89
CHAPTER 17. *The Conventional Loan Process* 91
CHAPTER 18. *Loan Participation Agreements* 99

PART FIVE: PROFESSIONALS AND EXPERTS 101
CHAPTER 19. *Accounting Professionals* 103
CHAPTER 20. *A Lawyer's Role* 111
CHAPTER 21: *Appraisals/ Appraisers* 119
CHAPTER 22 *Mortgage Professionals & Brokers* 131
CHAPTER 23. *Environmental Reports* 135
CHAPTER 24. *Title Companies and Insurance* 141
CHAPTER 25. *Realtors and Business Brokers* 145

PART SIX: OTHER IMPORTANT ITEMS YOU SHOULD KNOW 149
CHAPTER 26. *Credit Scoring* 151
CHAPTER 27. *Small Business Credit* 155
CHAPTER 28. *Construction Loans* 157
CHAPTER 29 *Start Up Business Loans* 161
CHAPTER 30 *Financing a Franchise* 167
CHAPTER 31 *Real Estate Investment Lending* 173
CHAPTER 32. *Sources Not Recommended* 179

PART SEVEN: SBA LENDING 185
CHAPTER 33 *Who is the SBA?* 187
CHAPTER 34. *General SBA Requirements* 191
CHAPTER 35. *SBA Programs* 195
CHAPTER 36. *SBA Fee and Interest* 203
CHAPTER 37. *The SBA Loan Process* 207

CHAPTER 38. The Right SBA Lender and Loan Program   209

CHAPTER 39. Apply For An SBA Loan   213

CHAPTER 40. Anatomy Of An SBA Loan Request   217

PART EIGHT: AFTER THE LOAN   261

CHAPTER 41: USDA Commercial Loans   255

CHAPTER 42: Not Approved   263

CHAPTER 43: After A Turn Down   265

FINAL THOUGHTS   269

ACKNOWLEDGEMENTS   273

APPENDIX I *State Economic Development Offices*   275

APPENDIX II *SBA Offices*   289

APPENDIX III *Glossary of Terms*   305

INTRODUCTION

According to the United States government, there are more than 23 million small businesses in the United States. They represent over 99% of all employers. Even with the present downturn, small business ownership in the United States is stronger now than any other time in our history. Women-owned businesses have steadily risen from 25% in 1980 to 40% in 2005. Obviously, with credit rules getting tougher, the trends will be more difficult to expand those numbers unless the small business community does a better job preparing their commercial loan requests.

Truly, it is the American dream to own your own business. Just as important as the previous statements is the fact that each year of the nearly one million new businesses opened only two hundred thousand will survive over five years. Most experts agree that one of the main reasons small businesses do not survive is the failure of the business owner to have the right amount of start-up capital, working capital and a good business plan.

Added to the above is the fact that if a small business is to expand, the need for capital is always at the forefront. Very few small businesses have the funds available to expand without the benefits of borrowing. It is safe to say that whether the business is in the start-up phase or in the expansion phase, the need for capital is paramount for success.

Primarily, this book is written for small business owners or proprietors who find themselves in need of commercial financing. I have found that many of the books written on this subject are too academic or clinical in approach. I will explore commercial lending from my experience gathered in over 25 years of working with borrowers and lenders.

It is a fact that commercial lending can be difficult, confusing and frustrating. However, if you have the knowledge of the process and prepare for your loan in an organized and well thought-out fashion you will have a much better chance of getting the loan on the best terms and conditions. I have supplied a detailed glossary of the many terms that a commercial borrower should be acquainted with and you should not hesitate to review any terms you do not understand.

I will begin the book with the identification of what you should know and what you should do before you even apply for a loan. I will lead you through the process of decisions you will have to make as to what kind of loan you need and then point out what you have to do to get that loan. Over the first part of my book, I will prepare you for the kinds of loans that are available from the low interest, good terms conventional bank loans to the private "hard money" loans that, at times, may be necessary.

With a clear understanding of the process, I will lead you to a very important section, the Small Business Administration (SBA) loan. It is noted that SBA loans are critical to the small business lending process. In many cases, small businesses in the United States would not survive without the SBA. If you are looking to open a small business or trying to expand one, the SBA is usually somewhere in the mix of the type and kind of loan you may need.

For other options for small business lending, I will offer advice on using government programs that are set up to help small businesses. Almost every state has an agency to help develop the small business model. I will provide a format and information on using these sources.

In another area of concern, I will give you some insight into the use of professionals in your quest for a small business or commercial loan. Whether it is legal help, accounting or commercial mortgage brokers, you should have an understanding of how to deal with those people.

Lastly, I have set out a loan project from the initial application through the settlement process. It will show you what to expect when you go through the complete process.

What this book is not about is stock offerings, incubators or large company lending. This is about small realty investor or small business lending.

Small business lending is not easy. Now, more than ever, in my experience an average commercial borrower needs help. The process can be exhausting, but if you can absorb the material presented, you will be better equipped to deal with the process.

I do hope you enjoy the book, take what I have learned, and apply it to your future funding needs.

PART ONE
THE BORROWER

At some point in your life, you will become a borrower. Unless you are born with a pot of gold, we all find the necessity to be a borrower of money. If you are already in business or want to go into business, it is almost impossible to be successful without raising money for your venture.

A business or commercial real estate loan is usually not your first loan. Most people who go into business have made at least a car loan, a home loan or have had a student loan. When you become a small business borrower or investor in income producing realty, you enter into an entirely new area of borrowing unlike anything you have experienced. Oddly, whether you are borrowing fifty thousand dollars or five million dollars, the preparation and commercial lending concepts of commercial lending are much the same. Since the average business or commercial loan is relatively small, I will concentrate mainly on the small commercial borrower.

CHAPTER 1
What is a Small Business Loan?

Before I get started, I want you to understand that this book is for the small business owner and for anyone who is interested in obtaining a small business loan or commercial real estate financing.

Are you a small business? It would seem like a simple question but like many things in our world, when we try to identify something, it opens up as many questions as it does answers.

When someone mentions a small business, we all think about the dry cleaner, auto repair shop, bakery and the many small businesses that are in every city and town across this country. In fact, the small business format provides over 50% of all jobs in the United States. While small is a relative term, it is necessary in most cases to define what we would all reasonably consider as a small business.

The Small Business Act states that a small business concern is one that is independently owner-operated and which does not dominate in its field of operation. I feel the key term should be, *"owner operated."* A small business concern should not be a corporation with stockholders, who buy and sell the stock for a profit. Families that would fall into our definition of a small business closely hold many small corporations.

For our purposes, I shall refer to a business that has less than one hundred employees for a service, retail or wholesale operation and five hundred employees for an industrial or manufacturing business.

Generally, these numbers correspond to the size standards for The Small Business Administration (SBA). Obviously, there may be other concerns, but I feel I have reasonably set out what we can refer to as a *"small business."*

Essentially, when we look to small business finance, we are looking for owner-operated businesses that usually need less than ten million dollars for either an acquisition or a refinance. With escalating real estate costs, along with rising construction costs, if a small business wants to build a facility, ten million dollars may not now seem like a lot of money. Obviously small business is a relative term but generally, the average small business is where the owners guarantee the loan and a small group of entrepreneurs runs the business.

CHAPTER 2
Options for Raising Capital

As previously stated, with every business start-up or with every business expansion, the single most frustrating element is how the business meets its capital needs. It is understood that most small businesses succeed by having a good business plan and executing it. Generally, there is a need for capital to carry out the business plan. I shall set out the main options for finding the necessary capital for all types of commercial loans.

A small business has two traditional main options for raising capital to purchase assets, expand or refinance existing debt. There may be dozens of different kinds of loan programs and methods of raising capital, but they all breakdown into two types, equity financing and debt financing.

What Is Debt Financing?

Simply stated, debt financing involves a lender advancing capital where the borrower pays it back by making a series of payments, of which part is principal and part interest. The payments are paid over an agreed period.

There are four major types of commercial debt financing: 1) commercial mortgages, 2) term loans, 3) factoring of assets, and 4) lines of credit. Added to the four is a special kind of debt financing, the construction loan. At some point, I will discuss how all four are used and the circumstances for the use of each method. However, they all have one thing in common; the borrower has to qualify for each loan with all the qualities a lender requires and to be paid back with interest in a stated period of time.

Types of Debt Financing

As previously stated debt financing consists of a defined loan against collateral or defined assets that result in payments made by the debtor to the creditor with interest. The following represents those common forms of debt financing.

Commercial Real Estate Mortgages

These mortgages, like residential real estate mortgages, the borrower uses a parcel of real estate as collateral and the loan amount is based on the value of the realty. With the loan-to-value formula, the lender relies on the income from the property to support the debt service for the repayment of the loan. There is an amortization period, (time allotted for repayment) along with a fixed interest rate or an adjustable rate, depending on the loan program. While similar to residential real estate financing, the commercial real estate mortgage lending is based more on the income production of the realty, rather than the production of income by the buyer or borrower.

Construction Loans

This type of loan is debt financing. The difference is the funding is used to build or complete the collateral in a time period where at the end; the lender is paid back upon the completion of the construction either with another loan usually a long-term debt (commercial mortgage) or the sale of the asset. Later in the book, I will go into detail of how the construction loan should be structured.

Term Loans

Sometimes referred to as *"business loans,"* or installment loans, the lender relies on property, other than real estate as collateral. Unlike commercial mortgages, the collateral is usually not one specific asset, but a collection of assets, such as equipment, fixtures and in many cases, complete businesses, which include good will with the other fixed assets. *Good will* is defined as that portion of value or assets of a business that is intangible and is the basic reputation or "good will" of a said business. Term loans have a shorter-term period with many not beyond ten years. However, where borrower has a long-term lease sometimes there can be longer terms. It is also noted that the lender scrutinizes these loans in detail than a commercial mortgage, since the value of the assets is greatly debatable and based on different criteria than a loan on a parcel of realty. As stated business loans or term loans usually have a much shorter term and generally higher interest rates compared to commercial real estate loans.

Asset Based Loans

Just as the words imply, asset based loans require a borrower and a lender to agree as to the amount of the loan against a group of specific assets, such as accounts receivables, inventory and other assets. Usually, the formula is straightforward and the loan-to-value favors the lender. Under this loan format the borrower pledges collateral, the lender takes a security interest and the repayment is not strictly based on the usual formula of cash flow and liquidity. The good part is that the borrower can use assets that are of value that are not being utilized. The bad part is the high interest rates and stricter terms. Later, I will go into the various types of asset based lending.

Real estate loans, by definition, are asset-based loans. However, the fact that real estate is considered very secure collateral puts the real estate loan in a different lending category or a lower risk loan.

Unsecured Lines of Credit

Like term loans, unsecured lines of credit are usually tied to unspecified assets or generally secured by a company's overall assets or personal guarantees of the major owners of the company. Realizing that the risk is high for this form of loan, only the best customers of the lender have an opportunity to receive this type of loan. In many cases, the loan documents require a borrower to have a certain liquidity to keep the loan. Usually, when this loan is given, the lender requests periodic reviews of the financials of the borrower. As opposed to secured loan transactions, the credit history of the borrower is more important than the assets of the borrower. Remember, the important factor is that the loan is given based on the borrower's overall liquidity and not given with stated or specific collateral.

Equipment Leasing

A sensible alternative to traditional financing for the purchase of equipment is the loan product referred to as equipment leasing. Simply stated, the lender (Lessor) advances funding based on the value of the equipment (collateral) and the borrower (lessee) pays installment payments to pay off the debt. In most cases, the lease is structured that when the debt is paid, the title passes to the borrower.

The difference between leasing and the traditional installment loan is the fact that title to the equipment does not pass until the loan is fully paid. This form of lending allows the lender to repossess the collateral without exhaustive court intervention, which lowers the risk to a lender. Usually, the borrower can purchase equipment with less cash injection since the lender will be more liberal with the LTV. However, with a higher LTV, the interest rate for leasing as opposed to installment purchase is usually 2% to 3% more and the tolerance for late payment is less. Since the lender can easily repossess the assets, the borrower must be aware of the need to pay on time. In addition, borrower should shop the various leasing options since there can be a wide variety of rates and terms.

What is Equity Financing?

The other method of raising business capital is through equity investment, with private investors, investment banking firms, angels or venture capital firms. However, it is worth pointing out that in non-traditional lending formats, there may be a combination of debt and equity financing. I shall explore that formula later in this book. Usually, the equity financing method involves borrowing from lenders who feel they deserve additional profits for extending credit for a project or venture that cannot qualify for bank financing or other debt financing. Equity financing involves great risk to the lender/ investor and thus a greater reward for making the loan is expected.

Types of Equity Financing

Raising money from equity financing usually involves a start-up company or a project where the borrower needs to add assets or equity to the deal for the deal or project to work. The borrower uses the projection of increase in value or income to attract a lender to the loan request.

Equity financing is actually attracting an investor, since the borrower surrenders part of the borrower's assets for capital injection into the borrower deal or company. The following represents the traditional equity financing sources.

Venture Capital

Usually the highest risk equity financing involves venture capital or a likeness thereof where capital is raised by a borrower based on an expectation of larger than average future profits. Generally, the capital raised is injected into the start-up phase where the lender provides the resources to take a borrower's idea for a product or a business to the level of production that the borrower can realize an income to payback the lender at a profit of over 50% within a short span of usually three to five years. Obviously, the risk is high, but the rewards are equally high. This form of funding usually has little if any collateral accept the business model or idea of the borrower, such as a patent or a copyright. When a borrower seeks a huge windfall, giving up a piece of the deal may be necessary. In many cases the only vehicle for the borrower to raise capital.

One fact to remember, the use of venture capital is usually relegated to key industries, like pharmaceutical companies, technology and many ventures far above the "small business" commercial model. However, the methodology of the venture capital can be used on a smaller scale to effect real estate development, small manufacturing or any other area where the borrower can show a projected huge profit in a short span of time.

Investment Banking, Equity and Hedge Funds

Somewhat like venture capital, the use of private banks, mortgage investment bankers and equity funds perform the same type of lending but usually tolerate less risk and usually the borrower provides more collateral, unlike venture, where usually, the only collateral is the idea or the business model.

In many cases, venture capital firms and investment banking firms perform the same function as banks with the exception that investment banks or equity funds use client's funds, raise private capital and assist with marketing bonds, etc. Once again, for the small commercial borrower, the investment bank can be a good source, but usually the loan request amounts are too small for their structure. Again, this form of borrowing usually involves a larger return for the lender or investor and it usually involves an equity transfer to themselves or their clients.

Hedge funds have become a popular means for raising commercial funds. While structured like venture firms or investment banks, they differ in what the word *"hedge"* has come to mean, absolute return or that the investors are more or less *"guaranteed"* a return. Not to get into too much detail, the hedge fund investor is usually a professional investor and the hedge fund makes sure they get a fair return that is generally agreed on prior to investment. This requires that the hedge fund counter balance its high-risk investment with less risky placements. However, hedge funds can be a source for real estate financing where a project carries more risk than a conventional bank will tolerate. During the present economic downturn, the hedge funds and equity funds have been severely damaged since the funds took on more risks than they had anticipated. I do not want you to believe that hedge funds are a good source of small business financing since the average small business loan is too small and much too conservative in profit taking to even appeal to the hedge funds.

Private Investors/Angels

An angel investor or business angel is usually an affluent individual who provides capital for a new business, usually a start-up. Where venture firms and investment banks require the capital request to be over a million dollars or more, angels will engage at lower amounts.

One of the advantages of the angel- investor- lender is that they usually offer their own experience as management, which helps the borrower with not only money but will also help with putting the business together or getting the business to the next level. Like all high risk lending, the angel investor expects a large return in five years or less. This option sometimes is available for a small business that has a huge upside with the right injection of capital. Angels prefer to have hands on approach as well as a favorable lending agreement. Many angels are retired executives who have the ability to offer advice and connect the borrower with other sources of capital. Largely, the angel investor can be a great help for a start-up or existing business that is struggling to get to the next level. Most states have angel networks where a small business startup can present their deal. Once again, the angel network is a tool for small business lending but not really main stream and usually only for unique business models, like venture and hedge fund investing, provide a large profit model with higher risk than a conventional bank or SBA lending loan request.

Comparison of Debt and Equity

Obviously, the main differences between debt and equity are the risk and the reward. In business or commercial lending, no matter what the loan model, the greater the risk to the lender, the higher the rate of interest, or the more equity given up to the lender or investor. Nothing proves this comparison more than when you are a borrower with little or no collateral, but you have a solid business plan or a terrific business idea. You must be prepared to give up part of your equity and or pay a substantial return to insure that you get the funding for your business or project.

To account for equity funding, the borrower should understand that giving up a portion of their profits to a lender is just another cost of doing business. The same holds true of debt financing. A borrower must account for the debt service as another element of the cost of doing business or an element in the business plan.

To get a better picture of debt and equity financing, please note the basic comparative differences between debt and equity:

Debt	Equity
1. Does not want any interest in assets.	1. Want a share of the debtor's assets.
2. First positionall liabilities.	2. Concerned with on debt.
3. Looks at hard assets.	3. Looks at growth.
4. Wants seasoned companies	4. Likes new companies with experienced people.
5. Not concerned with intangible	5. Likes intangibles assets, like good will.
6. Structured repayment	6. Investment paid back from buyout for pay back.
7. Low risk-reasonable reward	7. High risk-high reward

Mezzanine Loans

There is a type of loan product that combines both debt financing and equity financing. Mezzanine financing is a basic hybrid between the two that allows the lender to make a loan at a set return with an option to convert to an equity interest in the borrower's assets or borrower's collateral.

In most situations, the mezzanine lender will loan money to a borrower and subordinate or be placed in a second position to a loan already in place. However, the "debt" is not seen as a second mortgage because it is carried on the borrower's balance sheet as equity. In order for this to work the primary senior or first position loan will usually agree to treat the mezzanine loan on the balance sheet as equity, regardless of the way the loan is structured. In addition, the mezzanine loan can be put in place prior to the primary or first position financing.

The mezzanine loan usually will allow the borrower the option to present to the primary lender a loan request with a better LTV. The key to a borrower using mezzanine lending is that the mezzanine lender agrees to being treated like an equity investor and agrees to be paid after the primary loan is fully satisfied.

Now, in return, the mezzanine lender will expect a high return, with higher fees. Usually, the interest will be over 10% or more. However, the return is not as high as venture capital. This form of financing is usually available for an experienced borrower, with a record of accomplishment and based on a borrower's sound business model. Traditional mezzanine loans are made primarily in real estate development, rather than standard business-only lending situations.

Noteworthy

- In order to raise money for a small business, the process of using debt financing allows the business to avoid giving up an equity interest by leveraging the assets.
- If you want to use equity to raise money, you have to be prepared to show an investor large profits.
- Be familiar with all of the types of debt financing in order to decide which form of financing is best for your borrowing needs.
- Equity financing, hedge funds and investment banks are not common forms of financing portals for the average small business loan.
- Mezzanine financing is difficult and usually out of the reach of the average small business borrower but is available than pure equity financing.

PART TWO
WHERE TO BEGIN

CHAPTER 3
Inventory of Your Finances

Many times, borrowers who need to raise capital or to borrow money do not know where to begin the search. I believe the organization and the structuring of all the items necessary for raising capital is the best place to begin.

The first thing you should do is to take an inventory of the assets and liabilities of your business or commercial entity, as well as your own personal finances. Whether you are starting up a new venture or borrowing for an acquisition or the refinance of your present debt, you should organize and be familiar with your borrowing potential. You do this by taking an inventory of your finances.

Before you apply for a loan, you should know as much as possible about how you stand financially. Unfortunately, many borrowers find out too late that there is an impediment in their financial picture that can turn away even the most liberal lending institution.

Now, should you find a weakness, such as a lack of liquidity, you can take steps to remedy the situation before a lender looks at your financing package.

As you begin to take inventory of your financial situation you should become familiar with the following items.

Financial Statement

One of the first and foremost items that you should be familiar with is your detailed financial statement. The financial statement sets forth the listing of your tangible assets and the listing of your debts to the point of finding your net worth.

The three basics ingredients are assets, liabilities and calculation of net worth. If you have a company or an operating business, the financial statement will be the main ingredient in judging the strength of that entity.

When a lender looks at a financial statement, the lender will focus on not just the numbers. Lenders look to see whether the company or owners have financial stability as well as the actual amount of the company's net worth. You should remember, most commercial or small business loans require a guarantor; therefore, it is necessary for you to submit your own personal financial statement as well as the company's financial statement or balance sheet.

Balance Sheet

Generally, the balance sheet is part of the financial picture that shows the financial position of a company at one particular moment. It is a detailed accounting equation of the company or business to demonstrate the strength or weakness of the company's financial picture. The balance sheet and income statements are the main tools for many lenders' decision on granting or denying credit. Do not overlook the balance sheet.

Trial Balance

Should a borrower make a loan request during the calendar year or the fiscal year of the company, the lender will request an updated financial picture. The trial balance or interim statement is the tool for measuring the current financial picture. By definition, a trial balance is a record prepared at any moment in time to prove the accuracy of the company's ledger. If the total of the debts and the credit balances in the individual accounts, the ledger is said to be *"balanced"*. However, as a practical matter, the trial balance is a simplified record showing a snap shot of the income and expenses to a specific date without allowances for tax considerations, such as depreciation. This tool gives a snap shot of the present business activity. Remember, the trial balance and the balance sheet should be detailed to the same date.

Cash Flow

Once you determine your basic financial assets and liabilities, you now must determine the cash flow from the source of income that you can depend on to pay the debt service. Since you will have tax returns you can establish a baseline for calculating cash flow. Generally, lenders will look to historical profit and loss statements and income tax returns for a gauge on what the future will look like. However, tax returns include items, such as depreciation and in some cases losses from other business sources that can distort the actual bottom line cash flow.

What I recommend is first chart the past three years of income and expenses. From that chart you determine a pattern of income from the main sources of income from your business or commercial property. You will have a figure called total income from all sources or simply gross income. Once you have your gross income, you then make deductions for cost of goods and you will get your adjusted gross income. Now, if you do not have goods you are selling, then your gross income and adjusted gross income are the same.

Once you determine adjusted gross income, you then deduct all of your expenses that are reoccurring, such as utilities and supplies. In many cases, there are expenses that will be included that are non-recurring, meaning usually onetime expenses. Some of this type of expenses can include extraordinary legal expenses, expenses for expert reports or expenses that would not occur on a regular or annual basis.

Now, when you reach the bottom line net income, you can now determine an important fact to consider when you are going to ask for a loan. Lenders usually refer to a this as the borrower's debt service coverage ratio or (DSCR). In general this is calculated by the following formula:

DSCR=Annual Net Income divided by potential annual debt service (principal and interest)

For example if the company has a net income of $100,000 and the annual debt service is $50,000 you will have a DSCR of 2.0. Lenders will typically request a DSCR of at least 1.25 or in other terms that the lender believes that the least amount of debt service payments should not be more than 75% of the net income. As you can see, if you can determine the net income and DSCR of at least 1.25 you are better able to determine your fitness for a commercial loan.

Credit Reports

One thing to remember is lenders either will inquire into a borrower's credit from the national credit companies or will use their own credit format. The credit report will give the lender information on not only the present credit rating but also, the history of credit use. Be sure to review your credit and take the time to make sure that the report is accurate. Many times, there are mistakes that can make the borrower look less credit worthy. Later, I will go into the credit scoring system and how a lender looks at credit. Remember, the main reason for a borrower obtaining a credit report is to assess the credit and to correct any mistakes or problems in order to show the true credit worthiness of the borrower.

Liquidity

One of the elements that is very important to the lender is the ability of the borrower to be able to absorb its current obligations and to handle unforeseen setbacks, such as in construction financing, the rise of material costs or running into a weather problem that can cause the job to extend and costs may rise above the estimates. Lenders look at the current assets and compare with the current liabilities. Should the borrower's assets and liabilities be close to a one to one ratio, the lender would feel that the borrower has not the proper liquidity to handle a potential problem that can arise in the course of the lending process. During the present economic downturn, the liquidity of a borrower is even more important.

In addition, the type of assets can determine the liquidity. If the asset is a receivable or a non-liquid asset, it is downgraded in the eyes of the lender. If it is cash, or equivalent it becomes stronger, again in the eyes of the lender. It is important to make this assessment early and if there is a problem, address that by making business decisions that correct the problem before the lender has an opportunity to review.

In many cases, the best decision is to check with your accountant or mortgage broker to determine their opinion on your liquidity. As you will find out, certain types of financing and certain types of lenders require different levels of liquidity.

Being familiar with every item above as it relates to your business or your personal financial status, will allow you to judge not only the ability to borrow but more importantly you will be better able to judge whether you will be successful at borrowing.

There is nothing more depressing then to apply for a loan only to be turned down. Many people borrow out of necessity, but more commercial borrowing is done to expand or acquire assets so if your borrowing power appears weak, you may have to adjust or change your business plan and the type, kind and amount of the loan request.

After obtaining the best information available on your financial capacity, you will be better able to make that final decision to ask for a loan as well as the type and kind of loan that your financial picture will allow.

Later, I will discuss what you should be submitting to the lender and what the lender wants to see. In the process of examination of your financial affairs you will accomplish maybe for the first time an accurate, well-reasoned opinion on your personal and business financial status. This may lead you to rethink your lending thoughts and lead you to consider whether even asking for a loan is the right course of action.

Noteworthy

- By inventorying your finances, you will be able to spot a weakness before applying for a loan
- Knowing your financial strengths and weaknesses will allow you to better judge the ability to obtain a loan and can prevent you from wasting your time in applying for a loan you clearly cannot attain.

BORROWER'S GUIDE TO COMMERCIAL LENDING

CHAPTER: 4
Determine Your Lending Needs

When a borrower decides to apply for a loan, in many cases the actual amount of the loan is not well thought out. If you know what the lender will actually consider as a proper loan amount, you will be in a better position to make an intelligent decision. I will discuss the various loan scenarios and recommend what you should consider before asking for a loan. Once again, the more you know about the lender and the lender's requirements, the better you will appear to the lender. Too many borrowers find out too late that the amount of capital injection they plan to put into an acquisition or project is too little to gain a reasonable loan on reasonable terms. What you should know is that in many lending situations the lender will not finance the closing costs or consider the closing costs as part of the loan for purposes of the very important loan-to-value formula.

Know the Right LTV

With the above mention of the loan-to-value or LTV in mind, the following will set out some guidelines to follow when setting up your loan amount.

Acquisitions:

In commercial lending, as well as residential lending, the general rule for setting the maximum loan amount is based on the contract price or appraised value, whichever is the lowest. For example, if the contact price on a parcel of realty is $200,000 but the appraisal is $150,000, the lender will base the loan on the $150,000. Likewise, if the same property appraises at $250,000, the lender will use the contract price of $200,000.

I shall examine the types of loans and what you should consider when setting your loan amount that gives you a reasonable chance of being funded.

Real Estate Only

First of all, if you are buying commercial real estate, you should consider not only the contract price, but also settlement costs, and any improvements that have to be made to make sure the realty keeps its value. You must remember that the lender will primarily base the maximum amount of the loan on the appraised value or contract price, whichever is the lowest.

If the property is in need of repairs, the appraiser will more than likely either downgrade the value or appraise the property as one that needs rehabilitation in order to reach its true value. If you are aware of the need for repairs, have the cost of the repairs built into the loan. In addition, you need to consider that any loan for realty will have settlement costs, such as title insurance, recording fees and possible escrows for prepaid items like taxes and insurance. Also, be prepared to pay for an environmental inspection. The environmental inspection and its consequences will be explained in a later chapter.

Again, remember, that the lender will look at the loan-to-value (LTV) based on contract price and the actual appraised value. If the appraisal comes in higher than the contract, the lender will use the contract price. If the appraisal comes in lower than contract price, the lender will choose the appraised value, over the contract value. Where this can become a huge problem is where the contract calls for an acquisition of real estate, equipment and goodwill. If you are going to borrow from a conventional bank, normally the LTV will be based on the appraised value of the real estate.

What does this mean to you? It means that you must make sure that the contract sets out the breakdown of assets and you prepare for injection of more capital.

As a borrower, you want the value of any contract weighted high towards realty, in the breakdown of assets. When you have an opportunity to read the SBA portion of this book you will see that the SBA 7a loan allows for an LTV against the contract price, but will allot values and LTVs to be broken down into each category of assets so the LTV is based on the entire project costs, including closing costs, not just the realty. This apportionment of assets and coverage of entire project costs with the ability to borrower against those assets is a very strong factor in choosing an SBA loan.

Business Assets Only:

Just as the real estate acquisition, the LTV will depend on the value that the lender puts on the assets. Normally, if the business has "*good will*" and equipment, as assets, the lender will make a judgment on the value of each and will loan accordingly. Usually, on used equipment, the LTV is at 50% and the business's "*good will*" is more or less based on less objective measures. At this point, the lender will consider the other factors in the loan package as critical. Such factors, as additional collateral, history of the profits of the business, and other risk factors will usually be considered in the decision.

Later, when I discuss SBA, I will show you how a "business only loan", a deal without any hard collateral, can get funded at higher than 50% LTV.

Refinance

The borrower, who is considering a loan to refinance either for better loan rate and for terms or to expand the business plan with additional funding, is usually in a better position to make projections the lender will find credible. Unlike acquisitions and start-up financing, the borrower's proven income production usually will dictate the success of the loan request. Once again, the LTV is essentially the same as the other forms of financing, except the refinance can usually get the highest LTV available provided the credit and other factors point in that direction. For real estate, the usual bank LTV will be 75% to 80%.

One thing to remember, there are unique situations when a borrower takes on a less than desirable loan in order to get into a business or acquire a valuable property. Many times this involves adding a second position loan, usually from the seller in a take-back situation. This loan can be a problem to refinance. In this situation, the borrower has to setup the business plan to show a better bottom line that can prove that the borrower can pay the additional debt service. In many cases, this means a sacrifice by the borrower.

Noteworthy

- Again, knowing your lending needs and the loan to value of lender's requirements can determine whether you should put your time and money into asking for a loan.
- Any borrower can benefit from knowing what is required for a particular kind of loan and whether that loan will work for that particular borrower,

CHAPTER 5
What Kind of Loan Do I Need?

Now that you know what your lending needs are, you have to decide what kind of loan or loan products are available for your needs. Largely, the type of loan involves the type of collateral and of course, the risk that the lender assumes. As previously stated, the average business loan is usually debt financing, as opposed to equity financing.

To begin with, all business and commercial loans can be separated into two main types. There are *"single pay"* loans and *"installment"* loans. In addition, there is an additional ingredient in installment loans, called, *"balloon loans."* Obviously, how the loans are paid back is the defining ingredient. Among single pay loans are promissory notes, bridge loans and many construction loans. The basis of the single pay loan amount includes the debt service and the fees. When you borrow funds, remember, the net amount of the loan that you receive must exclude the built in interest and the fees deducted from the gross amount of the loan.

Installment loans are those loans where the borrower pays back the debt service with principal payments on a set fixed amount over a set period of time. Most commercial loans are paid back in 15 years, 20 years and sometimes 25 years. Rarely, do lenders offer loan repayments of 30 years, except in a *conduit loan* format. There are some specialty loans, like some government-backed loans, that exceed 30 years, but those loans are not for the average business or commercial borrower. Commonly, most acquisition loans are installment loans where the borrower uses the income from their business or from the income of the property itself.

The *"balloon loan"* is when the loan repayment is based on a set schedule of years or *amortized* over a set period, however; the lender puts in a clause that after a set period of time, the entire balance is due.

For example, the loan period is amortized over 20 years at a fixed interest rate, but the loan is actually due on the completion of the fifth year. This allows the debt service to be lower yet allows the lender to change the terms after a shorter period, especially when the general condition of the commercial loan market has changed giving rise to higher rates.

There is also another downside for a borrower. If the borrower has not paid the loan on time, has been behind or has other financial problems, the lender can get out of the loan without having to prove that the borrower defaulted. Likewise, the borrower could benefit if the rates improve. Please understand that if the rates haven't increased significantly, or the borrower has been a good client, has paid the debt service on time, the lender will want to keep the loan and may not ask for an increase and allow the loan another five years. I have also seen the lender reduce the rate to keep the relationship with the borrower.

Below, I have set out the different kinds of loans that you can consider for your funding requirement.

Acquisition Loans

Briefly stated, using borrowed money to buy personal property, equipment, business assets, an existing business or real estate, the key item is that the title to the assets passes to the borrower and that the lender will be able to hold the assets as collateral. In all cases, the lender sets the maximum amount that they will lend and therefore, the borrower has to be prepared to have the cash injection for the deal. Most conventional or bank lenders require 20% to 25% in cash or an LTV of 75% to 80%. Also, since the borrower isn't in possession, the lender looks to not only the collateral value but also the projections as to how the borrowers will use the assets in their business plan and usually require the borrower to give details as to the projected income.

Refinance Loans

Refinance loans are funding requests where borrower restructures either their loans already in place or loans that add more money to an existing open loan. In this type of funding, title does not change only the terms of the loan change. Usually, this loan is based more on the history of paying the debt service and not so much on the future projections. Whether the loan is for income realty or a business only loan, the lender will be better able to judge the repayment potential or risks easier than an acquisition or construction loan. In many cases the borrower can use more competitive funding products, such as a conventional bank loan. The refinance, in most cases, are easier to obtain. Obviously, the payment history of a borrower is more important than the projections since one is a fact and the other a forecast.

In addition, a factor is history of actual profits, which can give the borrower flexibility if the company's cash flow slows.

Bridge Loans

Usually, an example of a *single pay loan* is the bridge loan. This loan product is used to bridge the gap between two transactions or two events that produce a final outcome for a borrower. Some bridge loans are installment loans, but most are single payment loans. Many times bridge financing is used by borrowers to acquire a piece of raw land, have it reclassified and approved for another purpose, which yields a greater value. Depending on the risk, bridge loans will usually carry a higher interest rate as opposed to the other real estate based loans.

As in most single payment loans, the lender's fees and future debt service are built into the final loan amount. Most bridge loans are for assets that do not have a built-in income stream to pay the lender. For example, the construction loan; the classic bridge loan is a short-term loan that is used to fill a gap in time between the sale of an asset and the purchase of another asset where the borrower has a gap between the sale of an asset and the purchase of another asset.

The bridge lender must make sure that the loan has an end game or exit strategy to take out the bridge lender.

Bridge financing can be very difficult to acquire and quite costly. The borrower must make sure that the bridge financing works in the overall scheme of the borrower's profit structure. The quality of the exit strategy or repayment plan is one of the most important factors. Usually, it is the lack of a solid, provable exit plan that dooms the bridge loan.

Construction Loans

Obviously, used for the construction of buildings or business assets, this form of loan is detailed from the amount of funding necessary to the amount of debt service that has to be accounted for during the construction period. In most cases, the *bridge loan* format is used where the loan is paid off with a single payment; from either a sale of the collateral or the permanent finance of the finished product.

This type of loan is usually interest only, the same as most bridge loans. Again, the loan is generally for a term of one to two years, or a reasonable amount of time to finish the construction. Usually, like bridge loans, the cost of the loan debt service and fees are built into the loan. However, the lender tries to make sure that during the entire process, the amount of funding allowed at any one time is in the loan to value range of 75% or that the funding allows the project to progress in its path of completion at a value worth a similar LTV. It should be pointed out at the beginning that the lender is faced with two values, the *as is value* and the *as completed value*.

Simply stated, all income producing real estate requires a commercial loan based on the value. However, the construction loan merely estimates the value when the construction is completed. Later, in the book I will discuss the evaluation of income from real estate under the commercial appraisal criteria. Unfortunately, many business owners or investors in real estate fail to understand that a commercial property is only worth what income that it can produce from the use of the property.

Whereby a business loan that is based on the income of a particular business (no realty included), the real estate loan is based on a formula of income (rent less expenses) to debt ratio from the particular type, kind and size of real estate. Remember, there is a difference between the business that operates from that location and the real estate that the business occupies.

Many small businesses are owner-occupied and used for their particular business. However, standing alone, the real estate as used as collateral must be separated from the occupied business. Remember, if you are buying a piece of real estate, you must show how you will pay for it from income derived from the real estate. This is the main reason that construction financing can be very difficult.

Business Only (Term Loan) Loan:

When a loan is made to acquire or refinance an existing business, that loan is based on the assets and liabilities of that particular business and the ability of the borrower to run that business. While real estate loans are based on the income and value from that real estate, along with other factors such as the credit of the borrower, the business loan is much more complicated due to the difficult evaluation process. When you want to acquire a business or refinance a business, not only is the income from the business scrutinized, but a larger burden is placed on the borrower. Since it is usually the expertise and hard work of the borrowers that makes the small business prosper, the lender takes a longer look at the borrower. As a general rule, the risk to a lender is higher in the business loan as opposed to the real estate loan. Also, the term or length of the business loan can be a problem. Because the risk may be higher, the lender will want to keep the term under or less than the usual term for real estate. For example, if the borrower has a lease for 10 years and no real estate in the loan, then the loan will be 10 years or less.

Further along I will examine the term collateral. This will give you a better understanding of why business loans carry more risk than a straightforward real estate loan.

Start-up Financing:

By definition, a start-up loan is a loan that is used to establish a new business venture or where the borrower is buying the assets of an existing business that historically has not shown a profit. Usually, the loan is for acquisitions, such as fixtures, equipment, renovations, working capital, franchise fees and other miscellaneous expenses. Real estate can also be included in the start-up financing. Since the risk factor is high, there will be many roadblocks to finding a reasonable start-up loan. Most of the difficulty comes from convincing the lender that the borrower can carry out the business plan. Essentially, the lender is lending money on the future projections of a business. Without a history, a business plan has to use other means to prove that the business will make sufficient income to justify the loan. Generally speaking the non-real estate based start-up is in the highest risk category.

Equipment Only Loans

If you have a small manufacturing company or a small business that needs new equipment for replacement of aging machines or will be expanding, the *"equipment only"* borrowing allows for flexibility. With rare exceptions, lenders rarely advance funding for used or old equipment. I have discussed equipment leasing previously, but traditional bank financing for equipment is usually based on a 50% LTV, usually for new equipment and where the borrower has a relationship with the bank doing the financing. There are exceptions where either the equipment has an unusually long lasting repair–free reputation or the borrower has an excellent business relationship with a lender whereby the lender feels compelled to offer more to the borrower to insure that they keep that relationship.

The decision on whether or not to lease or purchase can only be made based on the following:

- Is the equipment being purchase new or old? If it is old, what is the quality of the equipment?
- How much cash injection will the borrower have available?

- What relationship does the borrower have with a mercantile bank or lender?

I recommend to all borrowers to make inquiries to both installment lenders and equipment-leasing lenders then compare. Beware of all the terms and conditions, not just the rates and payments.

In addition, there are lenders who specialize in equipment leasing but be cautious. Most private capital equipment leasing companies offer expensive terms and have serious penalties for early payoffs.

Accounts Receivable/ Invoice Financing Loans

Although receivable financing and invoice financing are not typical loans per se, the borrower who needs to raise money may see the necessity of this form of raising capital. Traditional invoice and receivable financing involves the sale of the assets at a discount to a factor company, who collects the money for a profit. Usually, the sale of the assets will involve the borrower giving up a large discount and unless there is a desperate need, the borrower should use those receivables as an asset on the balance sheet to present to the lender when asking for a business loan. In some industries, this form of raising money is a normal business procedure, but not for the average small business.

There are advantages to this form of raising capital. It is easy to qualify. You can get into a program in a few days and it could be a continuous form of capital for the operation of a business with products that have a high profit, like apparel or furniture manufacturers.

You might ask why receivables cannot be used to pledge as collateral. It would appear that being pledged would make more sense rather than sold to a factoring company. The answer is, they can be used, but it is very difficult. Obviously, a business loan or term loan does involve pledging the company's general assets (non-realty), but for a bank to offer a business loan just against receivables is very rare.

Inventory Financing

This form of financing is used by manufacturers and dealers to raise money or to finance the purchase of inventory where the lender approves the loan on the usual and general principals of lending and credit. However, here, the inventory is basically the only collateral. This not to say that other collateral is not involved, but generally the loan is based on the inventory.

Obviously this loan is used by companies whose main asset is their inventory. When the borrower is a dealer or wholesaler for a manufacturer, this loan program allows the dealer to stock inventory to speed up the transactions from the time of the order to the delivery to client. The rates and terms are similar to factoring, except the borrower owns the product as opposed to selling the assets at a discount. Most of us do understand that car dealers, especially, use their inventory or *floor plan* the cars to carry on their business. Usually, the manufacturer sets the terms to satisfy the deal so the dealer will stock cars from the manufacturer. This does work with other types of businesses but many people call this system, *consignment sales*.

No Document Verification Loans

A real estate loan product that was primarily used in residential financing but at times in commercial lending is the *no documentation or limited documented* loan. There are small groups of commercial lenders who offer the same type of loan format. However, during the economic downturn, many of those lenders have withdrawn the product from the market. However, recently, the product has made a small comeback. This format is used by the borrower who needs a loan, but does not want to show the documented income on the real estate. Many borrowers own and occupy valuable realty, but their income is below the level that would entitle the borrower to a conventional loan or even a private banking loan. In addition, many borrowers are unwilling to broadcast their personal or company income tax returns. Traditional real estate loans require the borrower to submit income tax returns to justify their income. The no-documentation loan does not need the income tax returns.

The no-document form of loan usually will have a LTV of no more than 60 to 65% and carry a much higher interest rate. Generally, the borrower or guarantor must have a good credit score, usually above the 650 Fico score. Many lenders adjust the LTV and interest rates based on the credit score. Also, many of the lenders will only use this format in higher population areas. One such lender will not lend where the population is under 25,000.

Now, since the loan is not based on showing tax returns, the lender requires you to prove you filed your taxes for the prior two years by the borrower submitting a letter from borrower's accountant. This loan product is not very apparent with the present economic down turn but there are hard moneylenders who basically use this format.

Noteworthy

- It is important for a borrower to know what kind of loan is needed to judge the amount of capital injection and collateral that will be necessary.
- Since there are many types and kinds of commercial loan products, a borrower must decide which product is best for them in their financial situation.
- Do not take a "hard money loan" unless you cannot obtain any other cheaper or better loan product.

CHAPTER 6
The Business Plan.

In my opinion, probably the most significant part of a conventional loan request is the business plan. Remember, the business plan sets out how the business will make its profits and how the loan repayment will come from the profits. The business plan can also demonstrate the borrower's complete knowledge and understanding of the borrower's business. In a start-up situation, the business plan can make or break the loan request.

It is extremely important to prepare a clear and concise business plan. Try to avoid long, windy sentences. Always provide as much factual support for your conclusions. Do not confuse the business plan with an advertising brochure. Lenders want facts not lofty, unsupported conclusions.

Now, since a business plan is a written statement that sets out how the business is set up to make a profit, you must be specific and detailed. Your plan should contain the following items:

Executive Summary

An executive summary is a short, concise breakdown of the business venture. It should contain an overall definition of the services, products sold or items manufactured. In plain terms, this section outlines the basic company's business. You should include a brief summary for the reason for the business plan or loan request. You should briefly explain the use of the funds for loan proceeds. Lastly, a general overall showing of how you will be able to pay the loan back. Make sure you are concise and to the point, while making sure you cover the above topics.

Resumes of Borrowers

What is extremely important to a lender is the background, education and experience of all the borrowers. Whether the business plan is to be used for obtaining a loan or for attracting investors, the plan should provide comfort to the lender or investor that the people who will be running the operation have the ability to execute the plan's priorities. If the business is a technical company, the borrowers must be able to show that the borrowers or the managers have the technological background necessary to carry out the plan. One area that the borrower should emphasis in writing a resume is the entrepreneurial background or prior experience with either opening a business or managing a business. Lenders tend to believe that a person, who has been able to run a business successfully, probably is a better risk than a person with little or no real experience as a business owner. Too many borrowers overlook the need for a detailed, well-written resume.

Resume of Management

Like the above, the background and experience of the hands-on personnel is extremely important. This is especially true if the borrowers are more or less investors. In certain industries, like the restaurant and hospitality industry, the need for highly trained and experienced management is a necessity for a lender to feel comfortable loaning money. Many times I have found that a lender will not approve a loan unless the borrower offers a key management person a part of the ownership. Many times this will require that key management person also join in the loan.

Description of Products and Services

Obliviously it extremely important to describe in detail how the business or borrower makes its money. Each product or service should be outlined. It should show the overall abilities of the borrower to produce a profit and how the business will operates or will operate to make a profit. If the borrower is a manufacturing business, set out the type and kind of products, the markup and the overall price of the goods manufactured.

For example, if the plan is for a restaurant, you must set out your average food costs and menu prices with factual or historical evidence. Remember, lenders have reference materials that show industry standards for markups, etc.

Company Facilities and Locations

Set forth the real estate, buildings or locations owned by the borrower or company. In many cases, these locations are also collateral; therefore the description should be in such detail to help the lender appreciate the value. If possible, color pictures or a short visual presentation can be beneficial. If there is a recent appraisal, it can help to provide it to the lender. Also, if you have an old appraisal, show the lender any changes made or any improvements made to the facility.

Marketing Plan

To bolster the projected profit forecast, the borrower should set forth the marketing plan or the advertising plan. Essential to a business plan is to set out what measures will be taken to market or sell the services or the goods of the borrower's business. A professional marketing plan will target the customers and should show how the borrower will reach them. A good business plan sets forth the background information on the markets for the borrower's business, the methods used to reach the customers and the budget necessary to carry out the plan. Especially in start-ups, a marketing plan involves an opening promotional budget and a monthly and yearly marketing budget.

Competition

Along with marketing comes competition. The plan should detail the main competitors of the borrower. Depending on the business of the borrower, the plan should include a comparison on pricing, service or location. If possible, attach what marketing information you have on all competitors and emphasize the borrower's claims of superiority or advantages. In many cases point out that the competition can be a help. Especially in the retail or restaurant business, a very popular competitor generates traffic that can help the borrower.

Cash Flow Projections

A specific area that is extremely important is the financial projections or cash flow projections. If the business is in existence, one year of cash flow is usually included. The fact that the company has a track record or history gives the projections credibility. If the business plan is a start-up or a major expansion, then the credibility of the projections become a major area of interest by a lender.

Remember, the start-up plan has to show the income stream that the borrower will be using to demonstrate how the debt service will be repaid. With a start-up, the need for a credible cash flow projection is paramount. It is not enough to state the income or sales projections. It is necessary to show how you have arrived at the projections. The lender will have a better level of comfort with a borrower who has either owned or worked in the business type that is requesting funding.

If the business plan is for an acquisition of an existing business or refinance then the basis of the projections can come from the tax returns and financial information of the existing business. With existing information the burden shifts to the borrower to show that the borrower can competently handle the management of the business insuring that the acquired business will continue to generate the projected income and the borrower can stay within the guidelines of the expenses anticipated.

Financials

Previously, I have set out that the financials should be included in the loan request. Some experts find it appropriate to include the business financials in the business plan as an exhibit, while others feel the business plan should not include the actual financials, but they should be included in the loan request. I see no real difference.

If the business plan is for an existing business, then the past two years tax returns should be included, along with the company's balance sheet and trial balance for the present year. Hopefully, the tax returns and other company documents will be presented in a proper fashion, using usual and well-regarded methodology.

Is a Business Plan Always Necessary?

Obviously, you can see that a loan request and a business plan can overlap and be duplicative. However, it is my opinion that unless the loan is so simple and direct a business plan is always necessary.

Noteworthy

- Besides the credit worthiness of a borrower, the business plan and the ability to explain the way the borrower will pay back the loan is the next most important factor.
- The business plan should be based on facts and not be merely an advertising brochure.
- If in doubt, hire an expert to write the plan.

CHAPTER 7
Preparing the Loan Package

To begin with, depending on the type of loan and the lender, the loan packages can differ. For example, if the loan is to purchase an income producing property, there is not a need for a business plan, but in its place the borrower should have a management plan. The plan should include details on how the borrower will be handling leasing, repairs and the other needs that a good property manager would do.

Now, if the property will be owner-occupied by the borrower's business, this will require a business plan for the borrower's business. If the loan is to be paid back from the rents or income from the asset, then the lender will want a management plan. However, many lenders have a mandatory list of items that they prefer to be included in a loan package. Usually, all lenders will request the same information, but many want you to use their own forms.

The fundamental rule in preparing a loan package is to assemble the factual basis to support a loan that has a reasonable business strategy. You must prove that the loan will produce a desired business result. In so many words, the borrower has to show that the loan works. While this sounds easy, in the final analysis, the lender approves the loan based on whether the lender has the reasonable and appropriate confidence that the loan will be paid back without default.

Simply stated, the borrower should set out to provide in an orderly and intelligent manner the credible facts, backed up by appropriate documentation to give the lender a comfort level with the borrower showing that the loan should be funded.

Using the above rules, you begin by looking at what generally is needed and then add to that package with the various items that your particular type of loan requires. Also, not all lenders need the same items. For example, the *no documented* or *limited documented lenders* (asset based lender programs) who base their loan criteria only on credit and appraised values, do not need a business plan, income projections or in most situations income tax returns.

Below I set out what I believe you will need for a standard commercial loan application.

Loan Package Checklist:

- Loan Summary
- Use of Funds Summary
- Resume of all Borrowers
- Financial Statements of all Borrowers
- Business Plan or Management plan
- History of Business Enterprise
- Financials of Existing Business Enterprise
- Tax returns for borrowers/ guarantors and business entity
- Miscellaneous information that can give the lender comfort with the loan request and the borrower.

Loan Summary

Even where the lender has a formal application, it is more productive to set forth a general statement of the loan request. The borrower should begin with setting out in a simple well thought-out structure the reason for the loan. Depending on the type of loan, it helps to have a guide for the lender to follow. The simple loan demands a simple executive summary while the more complex loan request, like a start-up loan, demands more information and data.

You should avoid long-winded proposals where you go on and on about every aspect of loan and go beyond the simple explanation for the loan. Likewise, you should make sure that at the least, the summary includes who you are, why you need a loan and what you will be doing with the money. Always be sure to include in the summary the loan amount that you will be requesting.

It is important to know that some lenders may not read the entire loan proposal. Therefore, your summary is very important to set a favorable tone so that the lender takes an interest in what you have to say. Make sure you put into the opening remarks enough of your strong points so the lender starts off with a positive view of the loan.

Use of Funds Summary

There is a fundamental need to explain how the borrower will use the funding from the loan. For example, if you are buying a business or realty, set forth the terms of the sale and make sure you attach a copy of the contract. If it is a refinance, explain the reasons and include information on the present loan that is being refinanced. If possible, breakdown the loan amount into the specific details. If the loan is for a start-up, identify the categories, such as acquisition of real estate, working capital, renovations or the purchase of equipment. You should remember the use of the funds should have a direct link to the profits or how the funding will impact on the profits of your venture.

Resumes of All Borrowers

Sometimes in the middle of putting together financial projections, collateral and business plans the borrower's background is neglected or over looked. Putting a positive face on a loan is sometimes the difference between being turned down and being approved. The education, competence and experience of a borrower can give great comfort to a lender where the funding request may not be as strong as it should be.

Make sure you include the following:

- Work experience.
- Education, including of any degrees or certifications.
- Prior accomplishments include any awards you may have received.

In this world of massive information outlets, the accuracy of any statements made in the resume that prove to be untrue or overly exaggerated can lead a lender to disqualify the loan for that reason alone. An example is where a borrower claims that he or she opened a successful business years before the present loan request and the lender discovers that the business went into bankruptcy. While it isn't necessary to put in any negatives, it does help to point out a problem and discuss that situation if it pertains to the present loan request. Remember, lenders have great resources and it will not look positive on a loan request if they find out a glaring negative that you should have disclosed and explained. As set forth above where the borrower had a bankruptcy, it makes more sense for the borrower to acquaint the lender with the circumstances. In many cases, the borrower can show that the bankruptcy was not from the incompetence of the borrower; it was the circumstances of the business climate, receivable collection problems or other circumstances out of the control of the borrower. I would hesitate to make excuses for prior business problems unless you have a substantial amount of evidence to support your position.

Financial Statements of all Borrowers

Extremely important is an accurate and detailed financial statement for all those who are going to be a borrower or guarantor of the loan. Many lenders require that any participant who owns at least 10% or in some case 20% percent of the business sign on as a borrower or guarantor.

As previously discussed, the financial statement is used to gage the net worth of the borrower. It also shows the liquidity and the kinds of assets and liabilities of the borrower. It should be noted that a borrower should not over value assets or leave out liabilities. Once again, lenders have the resources to check the accuracy of financial statements and any purported intentional inaccuracy can lead a lender to disqualify the loan.

Most lenders will request a personal financial statement along with the business's balance sheet, even if only the business is making the loan request. Also, avoid a poor presentation. A sloppy financial statement where the borrower shows a lack of fundamental understanding of the financial statement will again leave a lender less than enthusiastic. If at all possible, have a professional prepare the statement. It will have a professional look and leave the lender with a better overall impression.

Business Plan or Management Plan

Since I have already acquainted you with the business plan, you should make sure that your plan is comprehensive, accurate and based on reasonable assumptions. Management plans are used if your loan is for an investment property. You must set out in your management plan the following:

- The person(s) who will be responsible for the leasing, maintenance and management of the property. Set out what qualifications and experience of the important management people.
- Show the projected income and expenses in order to show the lender you will be able to cope with debt service, regardless of whether there is an increase in expenses or possible long vacancy periods.
- Provide a list of outside professionals that will be assisting you, i.e.: rental companies and independent maintenance companies.
- Copy of specimen leases.
- Rent rolls showing existing tenants, rent paid and lease periods. Always attach a copy of any executed leases by any of the listed tenants.

History of Business Enterprise

Almost like writing a resume, you should include the details of your business enterprise.

Always include the following:

- Nature of business.
- Types of products/ services.
- Customer profile.
- List of key customers, if possible.
- List of major competitors.

- Major accomplishments.
- How the loan will benefit or impact the company.

If you are not submitting a business plan, make sure you explain in writing separately the basic history of your business.

Financials of Existing Business Enterprise

You should present the most detailed financial picture of your business that you can build. You should be able to discuss in detail, any receivables and their age, the value of the equipment and any real estate owned. You should discuss all of the present open debt and discuss what company assets are pledged for any loans.

Once again, you should make sure that the statements are accurate, well prepared and detailed. An accountant or bookkeeper can assist and usually that can improve the presentation. Be sure all statements are done to generally accepted accounting practice standards (GAAP).

Tax Returns for Borrowers/ Guarantors and business Entity

Every loan request should contain the latest two years tax returns for all borrowers and for all business entities. For example, if the borrower owns other business enterprises, the borrower should attach the returns of those businesses, as well as their personal tax returns. Be on notice, if a borrower submits a self-prepared or hand written personal tax return and especially, a self-prepared business return, most lenders will not look favorably on a borrower, unless the loan request is small. One note, SBA loans require the latest three years returns.

Along with the tax returns, the borrower should attach a year-to-date profit and loss statement or trial balance for any business entities owned or has an interest. Each business should have a corresponding balance sheet dated the same as the above profit and loss or trial balance.

Miscellaneous Information

In many cases there are special items that can improve the loan request that are not normally included the average loan request. This can be a report from an industrial or peer group, an analysis of a special industry or something unique to the borrower. An example is a positive restaurant review that includes the borrower or the chef of the restaurant business that is seeking funding.

Time after time, the actual presentation of a loan request means much more than it probably should. This does not mean that lenders put form over substance. It does mean that if a loan request appears to be lacking in professionalism and the loan request is for a large loan, the lender will have doubts from the beginning. Like food, sometimes the presentation can cover the lack of taste.

Also, beware of stale information. Make sure all of the loan information is current. Since tax returns reflect a year's activity, should the loan request come after February or March, most lenders will want a trial balance of all business interest as of the month submitted. Always be prepared and remember, it is a negative to have the lender ask for something that should have been included. If you cannot get an item or you have an item on order, make sure the lender knows that you will be forwarding it as soon as it is available.

Noteworthy

- Make sure you follow a responsible checklist to make sure you submit the correct information.
- Remember, most lenders have a format to follow to submit a loan.
- Always ask the lender for a list of what they want to see in the loan package.
- Do not submit a loan in a piece-meal fashion.

CHAPTER 8
Submitting the Loan and Interview

When you are ready to submit your loan package, make sure the package is complete, organized and easy to read. Too many times I have found that loan packages are not grammatically correct, sloppy and un-professional appearing. This kind of loan package does not help your effort to secure a loan. You should find out where you should submit the loan, address it to the proper person and make sure it is delivered promptly.

Some practical things you should know before submitting a loan package. You should be able to communicate with whomever you are going to talk to about your loan. It may sound like a strange request but too many times I have dealt with a borrower who did not have internet service. You should at least have a twenty-four hour fax number. It can make it more difficult to obtain a loan if the borrower does not have modern communication equipment. Remember, rarely will you submit a loan package that there will not be a need to have detailed communications with the lender or with your loan consultant or broker. It is annoying for a lender or broker to deal with a borrower who lacks the ability to receive information and quickly send information.

Now, when submitting the loan request I have found it appropriate and important, if possible, to deliver the loan request in person and try to have a short meeting with the loan officer. Usually most commercial lenders will want a face-to-face meeting and a visit to the realty or business. Like all business transactions, a borrower should make sure to present the best possible image and always extend the best courtesy. What you have to remember is the lender wants to have confidence in the borrower. The confidence extends to every facet of the borrower's business. All lenders want to have faith the borrower will be able to carry out the business plan. Some lenders attach more importance to the face-to-face meeting then others. I always tell my clients that the meeting with the lender is like being interviewed for a job. You may not be given the job solely on the interview, but you can lose the job with a poor meeting. The same goes with the lender's interview. A bad impression can kill the deal.

Noteworthy

- If possible, have a professional prepare your loan request and business plan.
- Make sure the loan request and business plan is comprehensive, yet not too wordy.
- Check the loan request for accuracy.
- Have a trusted third party read your submittals and comment on the strengths and weaknesses of the plan.
- Avoid the pitfall of submitting a loan request that lacks substance and resembles a sales brochure.
- Respond to all of the lender's questions promptly and with a factual basis.
- Have patience, the loan request period will always be longer than you expect.

PART THREE
THE LENDERS

CHAPTER 9
The Mysteries of Banking

Moneylenders have been around since the dawn of civilization. Historically, the first banks were more than likely religious temples of the ancient world. There is evidence that in ancient times, as far back as the 18th Century BC, gold was stored in temples and priests made loans to merchants.

In ancient Greece, the merchants used credit notes that could be cashed or used in other cities. Ancient Rome developed a sophisticated banking system, but with the rise of Christianity, the church had influenced the moneylenders to give it up and scolded them. The church felt that money lending was usury and deemed it immoral. Jewish entrepreneurs, free of the church's power, began to establish themselves as the bankers in Southern and Western Europe.

To a greater extent, the United States followed the European traditions of banking and as a matter of fact, the new country, the United States actually put forth a better-conceived banking system not seen up to that point anywhere in the world. While much of our banking laws came from our British heritage, the United States has been the leader in the world in banking, leading to the present system of commerce. Regardless of the resent bank meltdown, the United States banking system does lead the way in the world of lending services.

One of the mysteries is how and why commercial lenders make their decisions. Over the course of many years, I have been surprised, baffled and many times almost physically ill by decisions made by lenders. An understanding of how they work can help you through the loan process. Understand that banks make decisions behind closed doors and that alone can make it difficult to understand what they do in each case.

To begin, there are many kinds of commercial lenders. They can be broken down into groups based on the types of debtors they accept, the risk they will accept and the ways the borrower is required to repay the loan.

All commercial lenders have similar criteria, but as the different risks to the different lender changes, the lenders begin to separate into distinct groups.

Below, I will discuss the kinds of lenders, what makes them similar, and also what makes them different.

CHAPTER 10
Conventional Banks

When you think of a bank, you are probably thinking about a *"conventional bank."* By definition, conventional means, conforming or adhering to acceptable standards. Generally, a conventional bank loan is usually made with risk to the bank's investors or depositor's money. This means that the bank has a greater interest in making sure the loan is sound and the risk is low. Remember, when you give money to a bank, that bank is a trustee of your money. This means the bank owe you, the depositor, and the highest degree of care. Also, all conventional banks are controlled by banking regulations of the state where they are licensed or by federal banking laws, when the bank is a federally licensed or chartered bank. Since conventional banks must adhere to regulations and the banks are inspected and audited, there is a layer of comfort when a person makes a deposit and where the bank makes a loan.

Generally, all commercial or business loans are scrutinized the same way, using the same principals, but conventional lenders will make sure that the borrower and the loan itself conforms or adheres to the highest banking standards. This means that the loans will have the lowest risk to the lender. Since your loan is held to the highest standards, you are rewarded with the best possible terms. In most cases, the conventional bank loan is the best type of loan in terms and interest rates but in not all circumstances.

Noteworthy

- The conventional bank loan is usually has the best rates and terms
- Always try to prepare your loan for a conventional bank.

CHAPTER 11
What Makes a Borrower Eligible for a Bank Loan.?

The following is the basic criteria by which most commercial banks or lenders look at a commercial loan. Remember, the conventional bank will make sure that the borrower meets the highest level of scrutiny. Since conventional banks are more concerned with risk than other banking operations, the borrower must have represented the highest level of security to the lending bank. However, most lenders follow basic lending criteria.

Credit History

Obviously, the type and kind of credit advanced in the past has an impact on the lender's view of a borrower's loan request. A borrower who has had credit advanced and has performed and has paid the debt service will be preferred over one that has a limited credit experience.

Generally, the lender will use the credit scoring system. In a separate chapter, I will explain the credit scoring system and how it works. Credit and how commercial lenders look at it can differ from bank to bank, from lender to lender. Usually, the lenders try to compare the past credit history of performance with the strength of the other factors and come to a decision on whether the borrower fits the profile that the lender believes is appropriate for that particular bank and loan request.

An area that draws particular interest is whether the borrower has ever filed for bankruptcy. Many lenders arbitrarily will turn down a loan if a borrower has a previous bankruptcy within two years prior to asking for a loan. However, many lenders will judge the borrower's credit including any bankruptcies with all the other factors in deciding to offer credit or a loan. Knowing how a lender looks at credit can be helpful. What a borrower can do is to go into significant detail, the background and reasons for the bankruptcy, and the result of the filing. If the bankruptcy was the result of an event, like a medical condition or an accident and the borrower was not negligent in conducting the borrower's financial affairs, the lender may choose to ignore the bankruptcy. Many times a commercial borrower may have been forced to file a bankruptcy because of a third party that placed the borrower in jeopardy. After the terror attack of September 11, many small businesses associated with the aviation industry and air travel suffered and was forced to ask for bankruptcy protection.

Now, to obtain a loan from a conventional bank your credit should be at least good, if not excellent, without any bankruptcy filings for over seven years. Remember, the conventional banks offer the best terms and will only accept the lowest risk borrowers.

Collateral

Banks and all types of lenders require security for any loan. The security for a loan is called collateral. Regardless of the strength of the deal, the borrower's credit history or the borrower's proven business experience and profitability, a lender needs collateral. However, collateral will not make a bad loan, a good loan. Generally, conventional banks require the loan amount to represent at no more than 80% of the value of the collateral offered and generally they like 75%.

A question comes into this equation when a borrower wants to offer a series of properties, rather than one particular property. Normally, this is not the type of collateral for a standard conventional bank, unless the extra properties offered are in excess to the LTV.

For example, the deal is for a $100,000 contract for a parcel of realty. The bank will loan $75,000 or 75% LTV. To make the lender more comfortable, the borrowers will offer more collateral.

Almost any business asset qualifies as collateral, although the lender will usually set the value of that collateral and also the amount of credit advanced on that collateral can change depending on the type of collateral. As an example, take raw land. Most lenders will advance funds for the purchase of raw land and use it as collateral, but they will usually not allow over 50% LTV.

Another type of collateral for a commercial loan is a personal asset of the borrower. Generally, the use of personal assets is not a usual request for conventional lenders. However, all lenders will request additional collateral where where the overall loan appears to work, but the lender feels more comfortable when more assets are pledged.

Most conventional banks feel more secure with the pledge of cash assets, such as CDs and deposit accounts. Generally, banks will not consider as collateral, the "good will" of a company. Obviously, hard assets are the preferred collateral for obvious reasons. One thing to watch for is the value the lender puts on the collateral. Many lenders want the loan collateralized at 100%. Especially be aware that most SBA lenders will give you a loan at 90% of project cost but want a 100% collateral. This can be a problem for some borrowers whose loans have a large amount of working capital.

Character and Background of Borrower

Rooted in the history of lending, is the lender's overall view of the borrower. Needless to say, the lender will take into consideration the background, experience and education of the borrower and relate that to the kind of loan request to determine if the lender feels comfortable in trusting the loan proceeds to a particular borrower. Commercial lending requires a borrower to carry out the business plan in order to make profits from which the borrower pays the debt back to the lender. While credit history is part of the character of the borrower, the facts of the employment history and education are also very important. Things like criminal records and history of litigation can be factors. When lenders see a history of bad behavior or activity that alone can be the basis of a turn down.

Cash Injection/ Equity

Lenders look to the amount of cash or equity that a borrower has in a deal, or the cash that will be invested or injected. The borrower's cash input generally sets the tone for the deal. This not only has the effect of lowering the LTV, but it demonstrates to the lender that the borrower is invested emotionally as well as materially in the deal. As a practical matter, most lenders feel that the more attachment a borrower has to a deal, the more security or comfort level exists for the lender. Commonly referred to as "skin in the game," the more the borrower invests, the more the lender feels comfortable with the loan.

In the final analysis, the lender will try to keep the loan-to-value as low as possible by either making the rates and terms more attractive or in the case of a *no documented, asset based* lender, solely base the loan on the LTV without the requirement of showing documented income. However, the conventional lender uses all four major categories in the decision making process. By far, the conventional bank process is the most accurate in forecasting a successful loan.

Financial Statement Analysis and Liquidity

Depending on the type of loan and the duration of the credit requested, the conventional lender will look at the liquidity of the borrower. If the borrower is an individual or guarantor the lender will look at the financial statement and if a corporation, the balance sheet.

There are many definitions of *liquidity*, but for most lenders the term liquidity means the ability of a borrower to meet its obligations when they come due. It can mean the proportion of cash to the total assets and the ease at which the borrower can convert those assets into actual cash without losing any value. Remember, a lender wants to know if the borrower's business income drops that the business can survive and meet its financial obligations, like debt service.

There are three main gauges to look at when determining the liquidity or strength of a borrower. They are called *business ratios* and they compare the income and the assets with the debts. Lenders like to see the comparison of the borrower with generally accepted norms of successful businesses. Obviously, the greater ratio of income to assets to the debts will show the strength of the borrower.

Depending on the business format, there are many ways to judge the financial strength and weakness of a borrower, business or asset the following are three of the ways to look at a borrower's financial picture and liquidity:

Assets to liabilities liquidity ratio-this ratio is determined by dividing the total current assets by the current liabilities. For example:
Assets of $250,000 and liabilities of $125,000, the current ratio is 2.0

Cash to liabilities liquidity ratio-this ratio is determined by dividing cash against current liabilities. For example:
Cash of $50,000 and liabilities of $125,000, the current ratio is .40

Debt to equity liquidity ratio-this ratio is determined by the total liabilities measured against the net worth of the borrower. For example:
Liabilities of $250,000 against a net worth of $500,000 is debt to net worth ratio 2.0 or for every dollar of debt you have two dollars of net worth.

Also, in addition to the above, many lenders will also chart the following:

- Accounts receivable-shows how long it takes to convert a sale to cash.
- Turnover of inventory-shows how long the company's inventory sits before it is sold.
- Payable dates- shows how long a payable sits before being paid.

As stated above, depending on the type of business, etc., there can be other tests to determine the economic stability of a borrower.

Most lenders will use credit services, such as Dunn and Bradstreet to obtain their credit information and to find out the averages or industry standards. Since there are only a few ways a lender can look at the financial strengths and weaknesses of a borrower, the business ratios are very important.

Loan Officer

Commercial lendersusually have experienced loan officers whose only job is to work with commercial loans. When you set your sites on a conventional bank loan, you will be faced with dealing with the *"loan officer."*

Many conventional banks have a separate division that handles commercial loans. Some banks originate the loans from their branch locations using loan officers who handle all kinds of loans. The loan officer will be responsible for taking your loan request, discussing the various loan programs, asking for additional information and many times will be the face of the bank in the transaction. Like all people you meet in the workplace, loan officers can be dedicated professionals, inexperienced but helpful and then there are people who seem not to care or worse seem to hate their job. I have found that loan officers can make your life easy or difficult.

When faced with a recalcitrant or difficult loan officer, be patient, be polite and do whatever it takes to get the loan done. Too many times, borrowers feel compelled to argue or debate the loan with the loan officer. Please remember, having the loan officer on your side can help, but usually the decision is not made by that person. Also, do not be fooled by the loan officer who looks at your loan and gives you an optimistic opinion. Many times they are more interested in making you feel welcome to the bank and actually do not really participate in the deliberations of the lending department.

There are other factors that you should consider when dealing with a loan officer.

- Do ask the loan officer if there is anything that he or she can suggest that will help the process.
- Do not make inquiries every day to find out if the loan has been approved. Being annoying is never helpful.
- Do not show up at lender's office without an appointment.

- If you are turned down, ask if there is anything that you can do to remedy the weakness or can you change the loan request to gain an approval.

As I have said before, the conventional loan request is generally the most difficult to obtain, so understand that being turned down is not the end of the process. However, make an effort to find out what exactly was the reason for the rejection and try to remedy before going on to other lenders. Remember, not all loans are for conventional lenders or banks. It never hurts to ask a conventional bank for a loan. Over the years I have been baffled by banks and surprised at which loans they have rejected and which loans they have approved.

Loan Committees

As a borrower, you will find out that generally you will not have any real access to the actual people who approve your loan. Most loans are approved by a loan committee made up of a number of different people who sit on the committees. Your loan officer will usually be the liaison between you and the loan committee. Many banks only use committees for the larger loans, so if you have a small loan, many banks use the signature system. Many lenders have "*sign offs*" where certain loan amounts have to have so many signatures agreeing with the loan. Some banks have more than one committee, depending on the amount and the type of the loan. More banks are going to a committee system where the members are solicited with the use of the Internet. Private lenders use more modern methods, while conventional lenders still want the committees to meet in person.

As I have said previously, too many loan committees have members who are not really qualified to make a large loan decision. Many of the members represent a particular interest in the community; have an economic connection to the bank, usually as a large depositor or as an investor. As a borrower, you may be at the mercy of these committees and at the mercy of a loan officer who may be well intentioned, but does not have the experience to properly present your loan. Remember, this is another reason to present your loan to more than one lender.

Noteworthy

- You should always request a conventional if the LTV is 80% or lower and all other items are positive.
- The first place to look for a conventional loan is at a bank you already have a relationship.
- If you do not have a banking relationship, then try a bank in close proximity to your business.
- Sometimes smaller banks are more receptive to smaller loans.

CHAPTER 12
Economic Development Loans

One of the better tools for a small business is the use of an *Economic Development Loan* (EDL) and loan guarantees provided by state governments. Generally, the EDLs are made in conjunction with the state regulated conventional banks. While there are also grants provided by state governments, I will concentrate on the basic economic development loans. However, you should inquire whether your state has grants for your particular business.

Every state uses its resources, along with the federal government to provide funding to businesses in its state. The motivation is to foster new business; keep business in the state and improve on the job creation overall for the state. In my state, New Jersey, they call the programs EDA loans that stand for *Economic Development Authority*.

The basic types of state sponsored funding available to small businesses are direct loans, loan guarantees and supplemental or second position loans. At the state level, the agency that provides help is usually called the economic development authority or by a similar name. In Appendix One, I list each state and the respective agency that helps small business. No matter what your business need, it pays to look for help from your state.

Direct Loans

Many state programs set out criteria for a business in order to receive a direct loan. Most of these programs target specific industries, specific areas and usually are tied in to economically depressed industries and certain geographic areas. The direct loans are usually tied to job creation. Many of these loans will be used to rehabilitate an industry that the state feels is necessary for the state's economy. Lately, every state will help manufacturing, which is a dying industry in most states.

Some good examples are the loans for the purchase of equipment, facility acquisitions and especially for the cleanup of environmental problems. Many old industrial states, like the coastal New England states and the Midwestern states have industry sites in need of help with environmental cleanup. Most economic development loans ask the borrower to add one new job for a set amount of money. My state, New Jersey, will advance funding if the borrowers can show they will either retain or hire an employee for every $50,000 of funding.

Secondary Loans

In many states the economic development loans are with secondary (second position) financing. The formula is for the state EDL to give a loan that will be in second place to a conventional bank loan. This will allow a conventional bank to do a loan where the LTV is now lowered to give the bank more security. For example, the bank will require the borrower to put up cash, at least 10% of the overall project, the state economic development agency will give the borrower a loan for 25%, in the second position behind the conventional bank loan of 65%. This state loan will usually be below market rates and the combination of conventional bank rate and the below market rate will result in a very attractive and functional rate combination. This formula allows the participation of conventional lenders to take on a riskier loan knowing that the state will help reduce the burden to the borrower. Again, this type of loan is usually tied into job creation in an area that has experienced economic problems.

Loan Guarantees

Many states offer loan guarantees that allow lenders additional security for making a riskier loan. Like direct loans, the guarantee is offered to stimulate economic activity in the state, create jobs or revitalize certain under achieving industries or geographic areas.

Later, I discuss the SBA format and will go into the framework of how a loan guarantee works and how they are procured. While not the same process the state sponsored guarantees functionally work the same way.

I will not attempt to go into detail about the above loan products since an entire book can be devoted to those subjects. However, I urge you to use Appendix 1 to find your state organization that can help your business.

Noteworthy

- Contact your state government representative if you have problems locating economic development loan programs.
- Prepare for a longer period of time to secure a state or government loan or guaranty.
- Inquire with your lender whether they participate with government economic development programs. Many lenders have programs that interface directly with development loans.
- Most states have programs that target manufacturing industries.
- Constantly check the EDA programs for your state since there are new programs, some change and some are modified.

CHAPTER 13
Private Lenders

In contrast to conventional banks, all of which are under strict criteria and banking regulations, the next group of lenders is known as private banks or private lenders. The chief difference between conventional banks and private banks is the private bank is free to make their own underwriting criteria and have the ability to alter the usual standards of banking to accommodate borrowers with credit problems, collateral deficiencies or unorthodox loans. This is not to say that the private lender abandons the usual banking criteria, but the private lender can take on a riskier borrower and at the same time they expect a greater reward. Likewise, many private lenders can offer substantially better terms for prime loans since they specialize in certain size loans as well as certain distinct types of loans.

Most of the private commercial lenders are national in that they can offer loans anywhere in the United States and some internationally. Many of the largest lenders are private, like General Motors Commercial Mortgage Corporation and General Electric Credit. These are two of the largest and the well-known.

At the same time, there are many small private lenders who are commonly called *"niche lenders."* They specialize in hard money, bridge and no documented loans. The landscape is full of every type of private lenders who specialize in lending areas that conventional banks do not like.

Since private lenders can operate free of many of the constraints of conventional bank financing, they can fill the need for funding where banks cannot help a borrower. Many private lenders specialize in certain areas; such as, apartments or multi-unit financing, office building or other well-defined areas such as inventory financing. These are commonly referred to as "Niche lenders." One such area of funding that is dominated by private capital is the short-term bridge loans or mezzanine loans. While banks do from time to time under the right circumstances make bridge loans, the mezzanine lender is by and large private funding.

What separates the various private lenders from each other? Usually, the main distinction of private banking is the rate and terms that match the risk and credit level. Where conventional lenders offer the lowest rates, the private banks offer loans to higher risk borrowers with credit problems, or offer loans to certain types of borrowers or specialty loans, like gas stations. Since most private lenders are national in their business scope, they can specialize and employ underwriters and staff that have a particular knowledge in a designated funding area. Since this lender has this narrow loan appetite they can use their expertise to make a better judgment on the viability of a loan request.

When you deal with conventional lenders, the rates will usually be around the prime rate. In most cases, the prime rate plus a 100 basis points or 1 % will be the conventional rate while the private lenders will be at least 2% or 3% percent or more above the prime rate. In addition, the private lenders will usually ask for more fees and expenses, thus making the loans more expensive. However, as previously discussed, some private banking operations actually offer very competitive rates, but they demand larger loans and only give the loans to borrowers with the best credit and liquidity. Many of the better rates and terms are for loans of one million dollars and up.

Just like there are many diverse sizes and kinds of businesses there are many diverse sizes and kinds of private commercial lenders. This is an area that a qualified commercial mortgage broker can be of great service.

Noteworthy

- Always prepare the loan request as if it is a conventional bank loan request.
- If you have a difficult loan, try to find a private lender.
- Look for a lender that specializes in your type of commercial loan.
- Make sure you do not settle for the first offer but don't pass up an approval unless you have other real options or have a reasonable chance that another lender will do your deal on better terms.
- Usually, commercial loan professionals or brokers know the private lenders and can help you find the right one.
- Be prepared to pay more interest and fees for a private lender.
- Be careful when dealing with private lenders. They are not regulated and many do not follow the conventional banking rules on prepayment penalties, default clauses and fees.

CHAPTER 14
Seller Financing

What is Seller Financing?

Commonly called *"take back"* financing, the seller agrees to finance all or part of an acquisition by taking back a mortgage. Used primarily in commercial transactions, especially in non-real estate deals, the seller will usually offer the financing with a short-term balloon attached. If you recall, balloon-financing means that the term of the loan is amortized over a long period of time, like 15 years or more and the interest rate is set with the stipulation that the balance is due in a shorter period of time, like 5 years. Rarely, will the seller offer a straight long-term loan without a balloon clause.

Most take-back provisions are offered to enhance the sale of a business or real estate. The seller, who becomes a lender, takes-back a portion of the debt, but does so in second place behind a first place loan.

When "Take-Back" is Appropriate?

While there aren't any actual rules for *take-back* financing, the usual loan considerations are appropriate. The first principal is obvious. Will the take-back be an unreasonable burden on the buyer/borrower? If your take-back loan is overly large in amount and in interest, then it is not appropriate. Remember, many first position lenders will not allow a second position loan. If the first position lender will allow a second position loan, they will want to see the terms of any second place financing before allowing the deal to move forward.

If the combination of debt services makes the debt service ratio too high compared to the net income, the lender will not allow the take-back. Usually, the debt service ratio permits the borrower to borrow up to 75% of the NOI or net operating income.

For example, when the income from the property or business is $10,000 per month, the lender will allow up to $7,500 covering the debt. If the borrower wants the seller to take back financing, the lender usually will not allow the financing if it produces a debt service problem much over the ratio of 1 to 1.25 or 75% combined. It stands to reason that if the loans together result in a huge debt service, the borrower may not meet the payments on the combined debt; there will be a reasonable chance the borrower will default on either or both loans.

Also, the loan-to-value is considered. I have found that the take-back amount combined with the lender's loan amount should not exceed 90%. Rarely, will a lender fund an acquisition loan where the borrower has not contributed at least 10% of the purchase price. Oddly, this same philosophy is used where the seller gives a gift of equity to the buyer/borrower. Remember, the industry standard for the loan-to-value is based on the appraised value or contract value whichever is the lowest. If a seller and buyer are related, for example, parents selling to child, then most lenders make an exception. However, rarely will a lender allow a deal to settle where the buyer has not committed any funds to the deal. Almost all lenders no matter the type of lender want the buyer to have *"skin in the game."* Many lenders will allow secondary financing based on not only the above principles, but the quality of the borrower and their credit as well as other factors used to judge a worthy borrower.

What Rates and Terms are used in Take-Back Financing?

While no standards or rules are commonly found in take-back situations, the terms usually reflect the buyer making a concession to complete the deal and that usually means that the interest and terms are negotiated based on the willingness of the parties to get the deal closed. If the buyer is anxious, the buyer will usually agree to terms favorable to the seller and likewise. However, the common formula in the practical world is the seller gives 10% take-back to the buyer at or about the same rates as the primary loan and the term of the loan is 15 to 20 years with a balloon clause, the loan is due in 5 years. Again, the willingness of the parties and the practical aspects of deal making are the main ingredients.

Take Back Financing should be used with Caution!

I believe that real caution should be used before committing to take-back financing. Notwithstanding the usual tests of standard LTV and debt service ratio, the borrower has to look at the deal realistically, intelligently and should make a sound business decision. The buyer/ borrower should consider that even if the primary lender agrees, the decision to agree to a second position financing should be made with caution.

The key items to consider:

- Overall terms? Favorable? Not favorable?
- If a balloon is included, what is the real chance of refinancing the loan within the balloon period?
- Will the additional debt service become a reasonable burden?
- Are you paying too much for the contract if the seller is giving take-back?
- Can you rely on the seller's financials?
- Should you hire an expert to examine the business you're buying?

What to do When 100% of the Deal is Being Financed by the Seller?

Over the years, an area that I have seen as a major problem is when the buyer decides to acquire a business asset without going through the commercial loan process and relies almost completely on seller financing. Many *"cash businesses"*, such as gas stations, small pizza restaurants (without real estate) and business-only concerns pass from the seller to the buyer with seller financing. In those transactions, the seller usually represents to the buyer that the *"books"* may not reflect the true profits. Also, in many cash businesses, the seller makes it difficult to obtain financing for a buyer because of poor record keeping or even understated gross sales reporting. Without proper books, which show a reasonable cash flow, the seller will convince the buyer to pay a considerable amount in cash and then the owner will finance the rest.

As I have said many times, commercial financing is a difficult and a sometimes-frustrating experience, but one of the virtues of the commercial lending process is the scrutiny that the lender uses can reveal the weak points of the deal and in many cases prevents the buyer from making a bad business decision. I have had borrowers come to me for refinance of a seller take-back transaction or even when a balloon payment due and I have found that the terms were so unfavorable to the borrower that it was nearly impossible to get this borrower a reasonable loan.

Remember, many of those transactions are for cash businesses with the seller convincing the buyer that they will make more money than the books reveal. Unfortunately, many buyers do not get a good amount of input from their professionals and that can lead to bad business decisions. Many borrowers are put in precarious positions by taking a loan that is not scrutinized by a competent lending professional. Many buyers rely solely on realtor's advice. Many realtors may not be competent to advice on the worth of a business or piece of commercial real estate. Also, remember, the realtor's allegiance, in most cases, is to the seller and the realtor is interested in closing the deal. I believe that many realtors who may very well know residential real estate do not have the experience and qualifications to adequately review or value a commercial deal. So, please be careful before blindly accepting take-back financing.

I suggest that any deal involving take-back financing, especially for a substantial amount of money, the buyer/ borrower should make sure that the books and records are correct and that the financing and the deal itself is reasonable and make good business sense. I suggest hiring someone to review the deal, especially an accountant or commercial loan broker. Make sure that the terms work not only for the sale, but also for any future refinance if it becomes necessary because of the balloon clause.

Noteworthy

- Make sure any take-back financing will work with your primary goal of gaining overall financing for your project.
- Remember, the take-back financing in second position will usually have to be approved by any lender that will be advancing funds in the first position.
- Before buying a business or real estate with 100% seller take-back financing, make sure the deal is reviewed by an expert to determine the value of that particular asset or business.
- Always us extreme caution before committing to take back financing.
- As all loans with a balloon clause, make sure you have a well-reasoned plan for refinance before taking a take back loan.

CHAPTER 15
Interest Rates and Fees

Interest rates seem to generate the most scrutiny in commercial lending. Obviously, the amount of interest a borrower has to pay has a great impact on whether or not the deal works for the borrower and the lender. What is extremely important to understand is that the conventional lender usually has little room to maneuver when they set their rates.

Unlike private lenders, conventional banks demand the lowest risk loans, must offer the best possible rates to attract the best borrowers. To offer the lowest interest rates, the banks set the return that they receive just above their own borrowing rates.

Essential to the interest structure of commercial loans is the type of risk, the length of the lending term and the loan to value. The credit of the borrower is always a main ingredient in the risk and so it does affect the rates and terms of every commercial loan.

To generally explain the rates generated by the conventional banking system, you should understand that you have to look at the two basic ways a bank raises money for lending. The first is to loan money from the banks own resources or own acquired capital. This comes from investors through the sale of bank stock and the use of depositor's money. The other chief way is through borrowing. Banks borrow from the central bank.

In the United States, it is known as *The Federal Reserve System*. Terms such as prime rate and discount rate are used to determine the conventional rates offered to the banks best customers. The following are terms that reflect our banking system.

Central Bank/ Federal Reserve/ Prime Rate

The central bank is the agency that has the responsibility of overseeing the monetary system for a country. In the United States, it is the Federal Reserve. Control is usually done by manipulating the supply of money by changing the interest rates. If the Federal Reserve believes that there is a need to slow down the economy, they raise the rates they charge to their member banks, thus making the cost of borrowing higher. This should result in a slowdown of the economy. Likewise, if the economy needs to pick up, *"The Fed"* lowers the rates to encourage borrowing. At the same time, the Federal Reserve System allows for the issuing of treasury bonds or securities that raise money to loan to borrowers.

The prime rate is the basic rate that conventional banks charge their best customers. This is a benchmark for commercial lending. Most SBA lenders use the prime rate as the index for setting their rates. Historically the rates are used to adjust the activity level of lending. Obviously, the lower the prime rate, the higher the rate of activity.

Historically, the prime rate has been as low as 1.75% in 1947 and as high as 20.50% in 1980. The rate is published daily in the Wall Street Journal. The Wall Street Journal is generally referred to as the source of the rate by most lenders who use the prime rate as their index.

Libor

Another benchmark is the *London Interbank Offered Rate*. The British Banker's Association sets a borrowing rate, similar to the prime rate. Commonly referred to as the *Libor*, this rate is set each day for the rates that banks charge each other for borrowing.

Many commercial lenders use the Libor rates as the index for setting their lending rates. A good rate is four or five basis points over the Libor. A basis point is one-hundredth of a percent. Fifty basis points mean one-half of a percent (.05%).

Using the above benchmarks, whether the bank is using its own capital raised through investors and depositors or the bank borrows from the central banks, conventional banks use the above as an index to set their rates. There are other ways that banks set their rates, but the above sets out the usual method.

Fees

Banks make money by charging interest for the use of their money. In most conventional bank loans, there are other charges or fees that are required to be paid by borrowers.

One thing you should remember, banks are in the business to make a profit and the cost of doing a commercial loan by a bank is much higher than doing residential financing. Because banks and all commercial lenders have costs, like for underwriters, they must offset some of these expenses with fees or reimbursements. Depending on the type of loan, the relationship between the lender and the borrower, the banks will charge certain fees. The following is list of potential fees.

Commitment Fees- This fee is usually referred to as "points', which means 1% of the loan amount. Points are commonly paid for by the borrower and paid at the closing. Since conventional banks are usually the cheapest source of funding, one point or 1% is a normal fee paid by a borrower.

Environmental Inspection Fees-This fee is paid to the bank by the borrower, usually after a loan is accepted and before the closing. The fee is for the inspection of the property for any environmental problems. I go into more detail in Chapter 18. Fees for environmental inspections can vary, depending on the property that has to be inspected and the type of inspection required.

Appraisal Fees-This fee, like environmental fees, is paid for by the borrower when the borrower accepts a loan. Depending on the size of the loan and the level of expertise that the bank requires, the fee amount can vary. In Chapter 16, I will explain the appraisal process and the different levels of appraisers.

Legal Fees-Banks usually require that the borrower pays for the banks legal counsel. Again, the size of the loan can determine whether legal fees are required. It is easy to see why smaller loans may not require an outside law firm to represent the bank.

Title Insurance Fees- Banks will require the borrower to pay for the bank's coverage for title insurance. You should understand that a title company will usually issue a title policy to the lender for the lender's loan amount. Should the borrower want a policy, for the borrower's interest or the whole contract amount, the borrower must pay additional fees, above the banks coverage.

Property Inspection Fees- Almost all inspections of the collateral property, including engineering inspections, HVAC and boiler inspections are usually paid for by the borrower. With construction loans, the lender will usually require an inspection before any funds are released to the contractor. This inspection fee is built into the loan and each time an inspector goes to the property, a fee is charged.

Please remember, most fees are not negotiable if the borrower wants or accepts the loan. However, it is not out of the question for the borrower to ask that certain fees be waived and in some cases, the lender agrees. This is usually done where the bank really wants the business of the borrower and receives other considerations, like bank deposit agreements.

Noteworthy

- Most small business loans are tied into the prime rate as set out in the Wall Street Journal each day.
- Most commercial lenders will refer to the prime rate or the libor, but will set the actual rate on the usual risk factors that all lenders consider when setting their rates.
- Make sure you account for the many fees when setting up your loan. Conventional banks usually will not build the fees into the loan amount so the borrower must pay the fees, out of pocket.
- Make sure that when you agree to a loan the fees are set forth and are not a shock at the closing table.

CHAPTER 16
Private Lenders' Rates

As stated earlier, private lenders have more flexibility when they set their rates and terms. Most private lenders or private banking companies generally structure their rates to correspond to the securities rates, prime rate and in some cases the libor. However, at the same time, the rates usually differ wildly depending on the type of loan, the risk and the borrower's credit.

Since many private lenders have investors who require a certain yield, the private lenders rates can and will reflect the competitive nature of investing. When an investor has the opportunity to invest in a low risk product, the private lenders must provide an adequate return to raise the money to loan to the higher risk borrowers or to provide money for the higher risk deals, like start-up capital, risky bridge loans or short term financing. Without the larger return, the private money would dry up. Once again, the old principle of risk and reward sets the guidelines.

High Risk or Hard Money Rates

As previously stated, the risk versus the reward theory of lending produces an entire array of private lenders who basically set their rates squarely on the risk, regardless of the impact of the other factors. While all lenders consider the risks, the private lenders commonly referred to as *"hard money"* lenders, use their own criteria to set their rates. Like venture capital or equity capital, the hard moneylender expects a large return on their money. While most states provide usury laws that apply to residential loans, most states also set maximum rates for commercial lending where charging above is considered illegal and usurious. However, it is not uncommon for a commercial usury rate to be set at 50% interest per year. Good luck with that rate!

In contrast to the typical bank loan, the hard money loan is usually the last option for a commercial borrower. The typical hard money loan is usually short term, one year to three years, and is a single payment loan where the interest and costs are included in the loan. Interest rates can vary from 12% to 20% or higher.

The hard moneylender is usually presented with a borrower with less than good credit and other problems that prevent the borrower from obtaining a conventional loan. Likewise, the hard moneylender is usually provided with collateral that will secure a LTV of not more than 65%.

Essentially, the hard moneylender must make a larger return to offset some loans that may fail or have higher costs to collect bad loans upon default.

Fees

The private lender and hard moneylender will generally charge the same fees for environmental inspections, appraisers and other expenses as conventional banks. However, hard moneylenders charge substantial fees as points or percentages of the loan amount. Many hard moneylenders will charge as much as 10 points or 10% of the loan amount required to be paid at closing. I cannot state enough that a borrower should hesitate before taking a hard money loan. The consequences of these loans can be devastating to a borrower.

Noteworthy

- Before taking a hard money loan exhaust all other possibilities.
- Do not commit to a hard money loan for a long period of time. Make sure you have a reasonable exit plan to take-out or refinance the hard money loan.
- You should always have an attorney look at the loan documents in detail.
- Realize going into a hard money loan may result in a difficult time when refinancing.
- Make sure the large interest and the expense of a hard money loan works with your business plan.
- Remember, most hard money lenders are not very forgiving when you cannot make the deadlines for payment. Be sure you can make the debt service payments before committing to that form of loan.

PART THREE
THE
LOAN PROCESS

CHAPTER 17
The Conventional Loan Process

Every lender, more or less has its own method of dealing with a loan request. I will begin with the conventional lender or the local bank. Depending on the size of the loan, the borrower begins with either presenting the loan at the local branch, if the bank has numerous locations, or sends the loan request to the commercial lending office of the bank. Smaller commercial loans usually are handled at the branch level with assistance from the bank's commercial department. However, the basic commercial or business loan that we are concerned with generally will have a commercial loan officer. With our loan package prepared and ready for submission, we now look forward to the road ahead.

Usually most lenders follow a prescribed method to evaluate a commercial loan. I will follow a conventional bank loan.

As previous stated, usually, any bank loan starts with the loan officer taking an application, almost like a residential loan. Many banks use standardized forms so as to keep the process uniform. However, many banks will merely request certain information and assemble the loan application by putting the loan picture together. Obviously, the more a borrower is prepared it makes the loan officer's job easier. If the borrower uses a professional, like a mortgage broker, the job is handed over to a professional to work with the bank. Without a professional involved, the borrower should be ready to have a prepared package to present to the bank.

Should the loan officer believe the loan has merit and the loan appears to be one that the bank will want to do, a *"term sheet or letter of intent"* is issued to the borrower. A term sheet is used by a bank to set forth, informally, without any legal terms, the substance of the terms that the banks will more than likely offer to a borrower, should the loan be fully approved. The term sheet allows the borrower and the bank to have an understanding before the bank goes through the process of having its people work on the approval process. If the terms do not appeal to borrower, then the loan goes no further or is renegotiated. If the terms sheet meets with approval, then the loan officer moves the loan along for final approval.

The term sheet usually contains the following:

- Identifies the borrower and property or the business.
- The loan amount and LTV.
- The loan terms, including the interest rate and the payment period.
- Sets out all of the fees and expenses that the borrower must pay such as lender's counsel fees, environmental inspection fees and the type of title insurance.
- Sets contingencies such as the appraisal and the environmental inspections.
- Identifies specific collateral that will have to be pledged.
- Sets out contingencies that require the borrower to either supply to lender or perform prior to the settlement.

As you can see, the term sheet or LOI is an informal listing of terms without the legal language of a commitment. After the borrower approves the term sheet, the loan officer writes up the loan for presentation to the underwriter. This write-up can be crucial. Should the loan officer like the loan and gives a favorable write-up, then the underwriter will start off on positive footing. At this stage, the loan becomes dissected and compared to other loans of similar nature, national statistical comparisons, industry standards and banking financial requirements.

At some point in this process, the underwriter may have questions. Start-up loan requests are usually looked at differently than simple acquisition or refinance loans. With existing businesses that have financial histories, tax returns and profit and loss statements, the underwriter can get a better idea of the reliability of the business to support the loan. Obviously, the start-up business is much more difficult to evaluate and will take longer to receive a decision.

When the underwriter is finished reviewing the business plan, financial data and other information, there is a report either recommending or denying the loan. In most cases, the underwriter's comments determine whether the loan is approved or turned down. In some cases, the underwriter takes, more or less, a neutral position whereby the facts both ways are supported and basically allows the credit committee or senior lenders to use the report for their decision. Likewise, many loans are approved for reasons other than underwriting criteria.

For example, the borrower has accounts with the bank, has a business relationship beyond the loan request, or the bank feels that the possible potential business brought in by the borrower will offset any possible risks. A good example is where a borrower has collateral, money on deposit in the lending bank but the underwriter isn't sold on the loan. The senior lender or loan committee convinced that the bank will not lose any money will approve the loan over the report from the underwriter. Usually, this process requires a written memo setting forth the reasons.

After the loan comes out of underwriting, the amount of the loan determines what is next. If the loan is small, the bank usually has a procedure that allows the agreement of one, two, or sometimes three persons with authority to pass the loan for final approval. Each bank has its own procedures, and internal regulations that set the policies. On the larger loans, banks usually have credit or loan committees that decide the fate of commercial loans. Many banks have a credit control officer who is involved in all loans, except the really small loans. The credit officer will examine the loan with an eye on the borrower, where the underwriter is more concerned with the loan dynamics and verification of the loan details.

Credit controls vary from bank to bank and from small to large loans. The credit or loan committee is usually made up of a variety of members with banking experience or business experience. To be on a loan committee is usually considered an honor and is an important duty, however, the landscape of many loan committees is littered with loan committee members who in some cases are not as knowledgeable as they should be. Most banks put on their committees the larger depositors or businessmen and women that use that particular bank. This can lead to a variety of problems with loans that are not particularly cookie cutter type loans. The result is that many good loans do not get done for a variety of reasons unrelated to the merits of the loan. Hopefully, a strong loan officer will present the loan to the committee effectively. The strong loan officer understands the board members and can deal with the problems related when presenting a loan.

Provided that the loan makes it out of the loan committee approved, the loan is then sent to the legal department or to a bank officer to prepare a commitment to be prepared.

The Commitment

The heart of any loan transaction is the legal relationship created by the commitment issued by the lender or bank with the borrower. Most banks, as well as all types and kinds of lenders issue commitments that set forth the legal and binding terms of the loan. Since most commitments have contingencies, the loan is not a final binding agreement until all of the terms have been met or satisfied. Even then, some lenders retain their rights to arbitrarily change their mind and withdraw an approval. This usually makes it even more difficult to legally hold the lender responsible if they do not close the loan. Most commitments are truly one-sided agreements.

Depending on the size of the loan, the commitment is either prepared by the loan officer, bank officer or by a lawyer on staff at the lender.

As previously stated, most loans have contingencies, such as appraisal criteria; the basic loan commitment is a contingency contract that when the loan settles, the contract is fulfilled.

Across the spectrum, many lenders don't actually issue a commitment, per se. Many actually send a really detailed term sheet. Some call their commitment a *pre-approval*, an *application* or simply an *agreement on terms*. This places the borrower in a position where the borrower really does not have any real legal recourse if at the last moment the loan is not funded. This issue should be considered when a borrower decides to go forward with a lender. What a borrower has to remember is if the lender issues terms, as opposed to a commitment, the borrower can reach a critical point in the pre-closing stage and the lender may decide arbitrarily to take the loan off the table. I have found this does not happen often, but have had clients complain of this happening to them. In all the years I have been involved in commercial transactions and lending I have yet to hear of a borrower who successfully sued and won against a lender for defaulting on a loan obligation. This is not to say that it never happened.

Most loans rise or fall upon the appraisal contingency, regardless if there is a legally enforceable commitment. Set forth later in my book is the appraisal process. At that point I will explain how the process works and how the lender uses it. However, should the appraisal contingency be met the loan will then go for final approval and then onto closing or settlement.

Prior to having a closing or settlement, most lenders have a senior loan officer with the assistance of counsel who makes sure that all contingencies or conditions are met and then approves the loan to close.

Again, depending on the size of the loan, the settlement process can move along by either the lender's loan officer, the bank's internal or staff attorney or in most cases for the larger loans, the bank appoints an outside law firm to represent the bank. Usually, the borrower is required to pay the bank's attorney. Again, the bank's attorney is there to protect the bank.

Settlement or Closing

The commercial closing, depending on the complexity and size of the loan can be routine or a long and drawn-out procedure. In my SBA section, the settlement procedure will be discussed in great detail. I used the SBA closing to demonstrate the scrutiny, contingencies and requirements that go into a complicated closing.

No matter what the size of the loan or what the type of the loan, there are fundamental items that have to be done. At the core of the settlement process is the qualification of the title or ownership of the collateral, the execution of the loan documents such as the mortgage and note, the accounting and allocation of settlement costs, transfer fees. If the loan is for an acquisition, the transfer of the collateral to satisfy the contract must be done correctly and to the satisfaction of the lender.

When it comes to the duties of the counsel for the lender, it pays to remember that the lender's counsel represents only the lender and has the responsibility to protect the lender. This may or may not include protection of the borrower. This really means the borrower should be prepared to have legal counsel that will look to protect the borrower. While it is not unusual for borrowers with small loans to appear without counsel, I recommend that all borrowers, no matter the loan size, have counsel that is familiar with commercial transactions and business loans.

Lender's Counsel

In *PART 4*, I will discuss the use of professionals, especially attorneys. One area that you should be aware of is that commercial lenders can require that the borrower pays for the legal fees of the lender's attorney. A good friend refers to lender's counsel fees as "giving a person a club to beat you over the head." That may be an exaggeration, but when the loan requires counsel fees to be paid by the borrower, the fees are set out in the commitment and have to be paid, if you want the loan.

Now, dealing with the lender's counsel is another story. Obviously, if you have retained an attorney, she or he will deal with the lender's counsel. If not, you should be aware that you are at a disadvantage. You should take the time to read over everything very carefully and ask questions. Be sure you can understand and are familiar with the closing procedure.

Items that a Borrower Should be Familiar:

- Title
- Loan documents
- Settlement expenses and fees
- Credits due to the borrower
- Cash necessary to close the loan
- Settlement procedures in the borrower's state

Even if you believe you are competent and knowledgeable to handle your own settlement, you should at least take the time before the closing to go over the various documents in detail before the loan is closed.

It is my experience that most borrowers are not competent to understand a complicated loan without the help of an attorney. Later in my book I will discuss in detail why you should use an attorney for the commercial loan process.

Noteworthy

- Most banks routinely follow the same procedures for the approval of a commercial loan.
- You should always present a well-prepared loan package and you should make sure you give your full cooperation to the process.
- You should be prepared to have an attorney review all term sheets, commitments, loan papers and closing documents.
- Be prepared to have patience with the process. It can take longer than you might think it should, as compared to the more familiar residential lending process.
- Remember, the lenders hold most if not all the legal cards when issuing a commitment so make sure you read every document and have counsel before proceeding.

CHAPTER 18
Loan Participation Arguments

An aspect of commercial lending that can effect some larger loans is the ability of many lenders to agree to fund a loan and at the same time make an agreement with another bank or banks to participate in the deal. Simply stated, loan participation is when a bank agrees to make a loan to a borrower and either before or after the closing, makes an agreement with another bank or banks to share the funding, servicing, profits and liabilities of that loan.

Loan participation is commonly done when a smaller bank wants to make loans for a major depositor, investor or a loan that the bank believes to be low risk, but the loan is too large for the bank's lending practices. Most banks will not loan up to their maximum lending limit, but when faced with a good loan that is near or over their limit, will become a *"lead bank"* or *"lead lender"* and will form an agreement with another bank so that the combined assets of both banks can be used to fund a loan. This is a loan that the lead bank could not or would not do in the normal course of business, except with the participation of another bank.

Participation also occurs when banks form relationships with investment houses, insurance companies and institutional lenders. Some lenders will also participate with the state and local agencies such as economic development programs, special programs for job creation and other types of government-backed programs. The bank will participate with an agency, like an economic development agency whereby the bank will fund a percentage of a loan on the condition that the agency will fund the balance. This is especially helpful to allow a borrower to gain a loan with a smaller amount of cash injection.

For example, a bank agrees to loan 60% of the LTV on the condition that the economic development agency loans the borrower 30% and takes a second position to the bank. Here the borrower only has to contribute 10%. All of the terms for collection of debt service, etc. are contained in a participation agreement between the bank and the economic development agency. Most states have these programs to encourage investment in certain demographic areas or certain sorely needed industries that can help a state with job creation.

Noteworthy

- Without participation agreements, many small banks would not be able to be involved in larger loans that could benefit their best customers and their depositors.
- Participation agreements can occur between banks, investment houses, insurance companies and economic development agencies of state governments.
- The sophisticated borrower can actually bring together the different participating entities to close a large loan.
- Consider recommending a participation agreement when you present a larger loan.

PART FOUR
PROFESSIONALS AND EXPERTS

CHAPTER 19
Accounting Professionals

One of the more important professionals that a borrower needs is an accountant. It is recommended to use a CPA (Certified Public Accountant). Since lenders want at least two years tax returns and a financial statement, the presentation of this information is important. Especially, in the larger loans, a borrower should never present self-prepared tax returns. Many times, the accounting firm's reputation alone will lend credibility to a loan request.

Knowing why an accountant is important is a necessity. There are people who never use an accountant to do their tax returns. However, when you apply for a small business loan, you should always use an accountant or a CPA. The commercial borrower should be familiar with the necessity of using accounting professionals

Let's begin with the financial statement. I believe it is necessary to have a basic understanding of a financial statement and the degree of reliance placed upon such statements by the lender when applying for a commercial loan. For a business entity, the most comprehensive and relevant form of financial information is the company's financial statement. Financial statements are not all the same nor should they be perceived or relied upon in the same manner.

As I said earlier, a lender looks upon a self-prepared financial statement with a jaundice eye. The first and easiest assessment to determine the level of assurance of a set of financial statements prepared by the borrower's external accountant is to inspect the accountant's report. These reports typically appear on the accountant's letterhead, with the exception of public documents. The accountant's information normally precedes the financial information included within the financial reporting packages.

The first paragraph of the accountant's report indicates whether an audit, review or compilation was performed by the accountant.

The procedures performed under each of these types of reports are distinctly different. Many lenders demand certain levels of accounting reports before a loan is offered as part of the loan request.

Many lenders require that even after a loan is made that the borrower sends the lender certain accounting reports so the lender can monitor the borrower's business progress. You should be familiar with each level of assurance provided under each report before agreeing to the lender's reporting requirements. The following is a brief discussion regarding the types of reports, the nature of service and the level of assurance.

Audit

Most small borrowers usually will not need a professional audit. However, if one can be done, the borrower will certainly impress the lender or investor. An audit represents the highest degree of assurance to individuals or banks that rely upon the financial statements of a borrower. An audit is not intended to discover any fraud or misrepresentation. Instead, it seeks to ascertain whether the financial statements are materially misstated or not. An audit may from time to time uncover fraud or misrepresentation, but it is primarily used to show that the business records are accurate.

An audit for a company may include detailed testing of transactions and an analytical review of internal procedures. Analytical review consists of comparing balances or ratios for current periods to the prior periods or the company's expectations (budgets) for that period and understanding and explaining any material variances. The depth of information analyzed in an audit is more extensive than that of a review or a compilation.

An audit includes gaining an understanding and documentation of a company's system of internal controls. The internal control system is comprised of the company's method for monitoring and controlling the business's monetary transactions. This system encompasses policies, which are intended to act as checks and balances within the company's operations. An effective internal control system is intended to safeguard the company's assets through the segregation of duties. By separating responsibilities such as physical control and record keeping of the assets, the company may be able to minimize the loss of assets. By no means can an internal control system prevent misrepresentation or loss in situations where employees collude to circumvent the system of internal control. The auditor may test the system of internal control through compliance testing if they believe that reliance on such tests will allow for the reduction of other substantive procedures.

At the end of the audit engagement, the independent auditor (accounting firm) may provide the company with recommendations to help enhance and improve the company's internal control system. Lenders typically require a company to provide timely copies of the auditor's reports.

In some cases, the process of auditing may also include the physical observation of inventories or any significant real or personal property. Independent confirmation with both related and unrelated parties is performed to determine the existence and completeness of accounts, notes and receivables, as well as the balances and terms of any notes payable. The auditor, through the inquiry of the company's officers or other personnel, will gain an understanding of specific events that have occurred during the period the books were under audit. As a result, audits can be time consuming and expensive. An audit might involve a significant commitment from the company's financial accounting staff.

It is recommended that an audit only be performed if the borrower is asking for a large loan and where the main assets of the borrower are the operating statements, the profit, loss and income statements. With retail sales, wholesale sales and the other business ventures the auditor can rely on the movement of products with accounting procedures to monitor the process. It is very important that an independent source give the lender a detailed report on the business. This not to say a lender will reject reports by internal accounting personnel. Usually, the cost of an audit is well worth the trouble. It is a real positive for any lender looking to give funding to the enterprise. This is another way a borrower can prove to the lender that the company is a good risk and worthy for a loan.

Reviews

An accountant can do a less costly procedure. A review is substantially less in its scope than that of an audit. Reviews consist of analytical review procedures applied to the company's financial results. In a review, there aren't any detailed tests of transactions or testing of the internal control system.

The independent external accountant will obtain information regarding the company's activities through inquiries of ownership, management or their related staff. For both audit and review, the external accountant must be independent from the company for which they are providing service. Independence precludes the accountant from having a financial or personal interest in the company as well as preserving the appearance of independence between both parties.

Compilations

For compilation services, an external accountant is not required to be independent as in the case of an audit or review. A usual compilation consists of placing the company's financial information on the appropriate form of the financial statement. Many lenders have their own forms and they request that a compilation be put on their form. There aren't any detailed tests of transactions, understanding or testing of the internal control system nor is an analytical review procedures applied.

In many situations, a compiled financial statement would not, in itself, be sufficient to obtain financing. If after the review of the standard compilation, many lenders require additional procedures to supplement and verify the borrower's representations contained within a compiled financial statement. In some cases, the lender possibly requests that either an audit or a review be performed. A compilation of the borrower's books can stand alone, along with the borrower's income tax returns, to satisfy a lender to move ahead with a loan.

What is significant in using an accountant or accounting firm is the need for accuracy and credibility. Lenders look not only at the bottom line of all financial records, but also the manner of preparation. If the lender finds a lack of comfort or credibility, the commercial loan is usually doomed.

How to Pick the Right Accountant

My rule of thumb for picking any necessary professional is the professional's experience in the area you need and will he or she do the job correctly for a reasonable price. Seems simple? Not really. Too many times, I have worked with accountants who seem either too busy, too expensive, not experienced or lack the aptitude to help put together a loan request. As you have seen when you prepare for a loan request, the financial documentation is not only necessary, but also critical and thus it is incumbent on the borrower to take great care in the preparation of the request.

Book Keeper, Accountant and CPA

Choosing to use a Certified Public Accountant can be costly, but for some loans well worth the price. Where a lender's decision involves mainly the examination of the borrower's books and records, the quality of the record keeping, tax returns and the balance sheets can lead to a better chance for an approval. Many times a sloppy return or an unprofessional set of records can cause a lender to turn down a viable loan request. This is not to say that you need a CPA for all purposes. When choosing an accountant, follow the lead of others who you know have a good accountant. I recommend that when you talk to an accountant, ask for a list of clients and call them for their opinions. Obviously, the list you get will be made up of positive relationships, but that will at least give you an opportunity to talk with someone who is familiar with the accountant.

Remember, the *bookkeeper* is generally a person who has little formal training, but is familiar with financial record keeping. Most book keeping services are the most inexpensive alternative. They take the raw data and prepare financial reports. They usually do not offer anything beyond putting the records in order.

The *accountant* is a professionally trained person who usually has accounting degrees from college or professional schools. The accountant will usually give the business owner a professional accounting system; put the business records in an orderly system that will reflect a more professional financial picture of a business.

While a professionally trained accountant can take the record keeping of a business above the book keeping stage, the CPA will add the highest level of professionalism to a business. The Certified Public Accountant must past a rigorous state examination and uphold the highest standards of ethics. For this achievement, the CPA earns the highest fees.

Do not feel that the CPA is necessary in all stages of business accounting and commercial lending. In most small business lending scenarios, an accountant can provide the professionalism necessary to impress a lender that the business books and records are accurate. However, if the loan is large and the business loan is based primarily on the records and tax returns, opposed to real estate collateral, the CPA can be necessary.

Also, make sure that the firm you use, either an accountant or a CPA, has the experience in your special field of work. A restaurant business, especially, should only use an accountant who has that background. Retail businesses, wholesale businesses and sole proprietorships all have unique accounting needs and thus you should try to find an accountant who understands your particular business.

In special circumstances, like applying for a loan to start a new business, the accountant, who knows the industry or business, you are going to open, can draw from experience to help set up your projections, budget and the initial bookkeeping system.

With all professionals you will need, you should make sure you have the right accounting firm for your business and of course to help you with your loan request.

Noteworthy

- Make sure you know when an accountant is necessary for your loan. I always recommend the use of an accountant, but on some small loans, it may not be necessary.
- Do your due diligence in picking the right accountant.
- Remember, an accountant or CPA may make the difference in getting a commercial loan.

CHAPTER 20
A Lawyer's Role

A colleague of mine once said, "If you want to get financing bad, call a lawyer." I, who did practice law, do not feel the same way, but I understand what he was saying. Of all your advisors and professionals, your lawyer may be the only one who is always necessary. As you read further, you will see why.

I can relay a real experience involving an attorney that can best demonstrate the need for the right attorney for the right situation. I was working with a client who wanted to start-up a business and wanted to put in a contract on a piece of real estate. I had reviewed the preliminary business plan and financials and thought the deal had real merit. However, the client was having a hard time getting a contract on the realty. I had been talking with this client for over a month and wondered out-loud why the contract was taking so long. The client told me that her attorney was difficult to work with because when she had to talk with him, she had to go to a pizza shop where he worked part time. She would talk to him while he made pizza. I then asked why she used this attorney and she replied that he was her brother-in-law and was representing her as a favor. I did my best to convince her to hire a full time attorney but to no avail. The deal never did get done. Another buyer had presented a contract and it was accepted. My client was left out because of her refusal to hire a full time, competent attorney. A lesson learned but learned too late. I have called the use of an attorney that is a family member, inexperienced in commercial lending, the "My *cousin Vinnie syndrome.*"

Generally, your financial advisors and your commercial mortgage consultant or broker can help you answer questions about commercial loans, but in general, the attorney insures that the borrower understands all of the terms and conditions of the loan documents. The following is a brief review of the typical loan process and how a lawyer can help make the process a success and protect the borrower.

Loan Term Sheet, LOI and Commitment Letter

As discussed earlier, lenders will submit term sheets and LOIs or a formal proposal to the borrower that outlines the terms of the loan. It includes the interest rate and the repayment schedule, the security/collateral for the loan and the costs to be paid by the borrower. It is important to carefully review this document prior to signing and returning it to the lender. Since this document sets forth all of the basic terms of the loan, once accepted by the borrower, it may be impossible to change the terms at a later date should a problem arise. An experienced business attorney can help the borrower with this process because the lawyer is accustomed to reading all of the fine print in the loan agreement and knows where to look for the provisions that are significant to the borrower. Also, the attorney can negotiate terms more favorable for the borrower.

Loan Documents

The next step in the process is the actual loan documents, which will include, at a minimum, a promissory note and a security agreement or mortgage agreement. For the small loans, lenders typically have standard form documents, which do not allow for much negotiation. Typically, when the loan exceeds $200,000 or more, a custom drafted loan agreement is more common. Sometimes there is a greater leeway to negotiate the terms and conditions.

Some of the legal issues that you should be concerned with when negotiating the loan agreement are:

- The security for the loan and the collateral offered.
- Whether or not personal guarantees are required and can the guarantees be modified.
- Affirmative and/or negative covenants with respect to the operation of the business.
- The default paragraphs as it pertains to the borrower.

- Re-payment/pre-payment terms.
- Fees charged.

All lenders generally require some collateral or security for the repayment of the loan. The attorney helps the borrower secure the most appropriate security for the loan. For most small and middle market companies, lenders often require the principals/owners of the business to personally guarantee loans. If the business has adequate collateral to secure the loan, without resorting to the assets of the owners, the owners should not automatically agree to provide their personal guarantees. In addition, they should avoid having their spouses act as co-guarantors of the loan, particularly when the spouse is not active in the business.

Another provision that should be carefully reviewed is the definition of the collateral for the loan. The definition of *"collateral"* should match that which is contained in the commitment letter. For example, if the collateral is intended to be limited to a single piece of equipment, it should not refer to other business assets. It is not uncommon for the collateral to include accounts receivable, inventory, equipment, proceeds of insurance, cash deposits that the borrower may have with the bank and a mortgage on company-owned real estate.

It is important to be aware of the lender's rights and the business' rights in those accounts when there is a loan balance outstanding. Carefully reviewing provisions with counsel prior to signing the loan agreement can help avoid many potential problems that may be encountered later should things not go exactly as planned.

Covenants

Another issue where the advice of an attorney is valuable is with respect to any affirmative or negative covenants contained in the loan documents. Often owners of a business have advanced personal loans to their business. When approaching a bank or other lender to obtain additional financing, the lender typically requires that any security interest that the owner might have in the company's assets be subordinated to the lender's security interest.

In certain cases, the lender may also request that no payments be made on the debt owed to the principal during the term of the proposed loan or will limit the distributions and dividends made by the company to its owners. Among the types of negative covenants are provisions that accelerate the due date of the loan in the event that there is a change in ownership of the company. They are:

- If certain assets are sold;
- If there is the death or disability of one of the principals of the company;
- Or the catch-all phrase *"If the lender is otherwise insecure."*

The above examples of clauses need to be carefully reviewed to determine if they are likely to have any impact on the loan transaction and whether an attempt should be made to negotiate them out of the agreement. Should the covenant stating, "If the lender is otherwise insecure," remain in the loan documents, the lender will have almost an arbitrary right to call the loan due. This can be disastrous for a small business that may experience a slow or down period.

Pre-Payment Penalties

An area that should be of great concern to the borrower is the pre-payment penalty. This is a clause in the financing that should the borrower payoff the loan early, usually in the first three to five years; the borrower must pay a percentage of the remaining balance as a penalty. The classic pre-pay clause is referred to "5-4-3-2-1." This means, for example, if you pay off the loan in full in the first year, the lender receives 5% of the remaining balance as part of the final payoff. Then, if the loan is refinanced or if a sale occurs in the second year, the borrower pays 4%. Another, more onerous pre-payment clause is commonly referred to as the so-called, *"California Rule"* which during the first five years of the loan, if the borrower's pays off loan, the borrower will have to pay a fee that amounts to six months interest on 80% on the balance of the loan.

Now, you probably will wonder why lenders charge a prepayment penalty. The main reason for the prepayment penalty is to ensure that the lender will make a reasonable profit. There are a lot of expenses involved in the funding decision made by the lender. The need for at least a certain amount of time for the payment of interest is necessary to be able to recoup the expenses of all the hours of work by their personnel to examine the loan. Obviously, the lender should be able to know that a certain amount of interest will be paid in order to make a profit on the loan. An attorney can find the clause and explain it; hopefully, the clause isn't an impediment to the loan closing. I have suggested to many clients, that the prepayment clause can be negotiated; however, generally it is difficult. One of the only ways to remove the clause is to pay the lender upfront fees or percentage points of loan amount. Only if the borrower sees that a refinance will be in the near future should this clause be a worry. Also, the lawyer can negotiate a modified pre-payment clause where the borrower can <u>sell</u> the assets without having to pay the penalty but <u>cannot refinance</u> without paying the penalty fees. This protects the lender from the borrower continually looking for a better rate, yet allows the borrower to sell without paying the penalty.

Formation Questions

One of the key areas a lawyer can help in the commercial lending process is the decision by the borrower as to what kind of legal entity the borrower should use to hold an asset, either on acquisition or refinance. In many cases, the attorney can advise that setting up a corporation, partnership or LLC, can save tax dollars, escape any personal liability or for other good legal reasons. Remember, when a borrower is putting in place a large debt on a company, it is a good time to decide the legal form of the company and how the debt should be held.

Many small businesses start off in the wrong legal form and it takes an event like a large commercial loan for the owners to reconsider the proper legal form. In many cases, the lender will require a certain entity. For example, where a borrower owns an asset in their personal name and will be using such asset for developing a business, the lender will want the asset peeled off into a *"single purpose entity,"* such as a Sub S corporation. This new legal entity holding the collateral will keep the property free of any issues emanating from the personal financial issues of the borrower.

It is extremely important to have a qualified business attorney give you advice as to the best legal form for your business prior to making a commercial loan request.

Closing the loan

In my professional opinion, the attorney is vital to not only advising the borrower of the correct things to do legally, but to expedite the closing of the loan. In most commercial loans, especially the larger loans, the lender has an attorney to protect the lender's rights. The process of the due diligence of the closing can place a huge demand on the borrower. The borrower's attorney can work with the lender's counsel to make sure the correct documents are presented. An attorney looking out for the interests of the borrower can make sure the insurance is correct and can avoid any unnecessary problems that can hold up the closing. In almost every commercial loan, there will be a series of items that the lender will want reviewed. The borrower may not be competent to supply those items, making it necessary to have an experienced person to assist. The attorney can assemble and present to the lender the items necessary for a closing to occur.

Who Should You Call?

Too many times, I have had clients retain an attorney who has little or no experience in commercial lending. Many lawyers do not have a volume of commercial clients and therefore may not truly understand the commercial lending process. This is not to say that the lawyers are not competent, it's just difficult to have to watch an inexperienced lawyer slow the process to a crawl while he or she learns the commercial lending process.

My advice is to make sure that the lawyer you do choose really understands the commercial lending process. Whatever method you choose to use, the bottom line is to do your best to engage the correct attorney at a reasonable fee. If in doubt, check with your local bar association for their lawyer referral network. Generally, these services are a real help and worthwhile taking the time to make sure you have the right lawyer for your particular loan.

Noteworthy

- You should always have an attorney review your loan papers before you commit to a commercial loan.
- If possible, hire a lawyer who specializes in business law.
- Avoid hiring an attorney simply because of their inexpensive fees or the fact that the lawyer is a family member.
- Always keep the attorney up to date on important events and review all-important papers, etc.
- A good attorney may prevent you from making a bad decision and will protect your rights.
- If you do know of an attorney for your commercial loan, contact your local bar association's referral service.

CHAPTER 21
Appraisals/Appraisers

One of the most important aspects of obtaining a commercial or business loan is that in most lending scenarios; the lender requests an appraisal of the realty or the collateral. Unlike residential real estate appraisals, where in most cases, the mortgage banker or broker arranges for the appraisal report, the commercial lender usually appoints the appraiser and in such, the lender can set certain criteria and have more control over the way the appraisal is done. Also, the lender will have extensive knowledge of the background and qualifications of the appraiser, which will allow the lender to have greater comfort with the appraisal.

The MAI appraiser is a highest designation given by The Appraisal Institute

There are a number of levels of qualifications of appraisers. Usually, all appraisers are certified by the state where they work, but all prepare the report in conformance with the Uniform Standards of Professional Appraisal Practice as well as Title XI of the Financial Institutional Reform, Recovery and Enforcement Act of 1989 (FIRREA). Some appraisal designations come from training and experience in specialized areas. The designations have requirements that go well beyond most state licensing requirements.

The commercial appraiser, who is usually the most qualified, carries the title as an *MAI*. This group usually specializes in income producing properties. Some lenders require that all appraisers hired must carry the *MAI* designation.

The Appraisal Institute has designations for the appraisers who have reached certain levels of education and experience. While the MAI has received a passing grade on 11 examinations and 380 hours of classroom teaching, the SRA designation requires passing on 6 examinations and 200 hours in the classroom. The SRPA designation requires a four-year college degree and a passing grade on a series of examinations. Remember, the higher the designation, the more credibility the appraiser will have with the lenders.

APPRAISING REAL ESTATE

While there are all kinds of assets that can be posted as collateral, real estate is usually the most important and the most valuable. A fundamental principle in commercial lending is that the value of the property pledged as collateral should be greater than the loan amount. There are maximum loan-to-value (LTV) ratios for income producing property loans. For example, for conventional loans, the maximum LTV ratio is usually 75% to 80%. For income producing properties, in many cases the LTV may be 70% or less. Later, I will discuss why the lender requires a lower LTV.

In practice, the purchase price of real estate and the appraised value are, often, not the same. So, for the purpose of the LTV ratio, the lender will base the loan amount and LTV on the lower of the two numbers, either on the contract price or on the appraised value.

In commercial lending there is no other issue that sparks more controversy than the appraisal process and the methods used to place a value on realty. It is always a struggle between owners, sellers, buyers and lenders. Each has their own way at looking at the process. When you couple that with the fact that there are a number of ways to appraise realty, you have at times the perfect storm.

METHODS OF APPRAISALS

There are three major methods of appraising real estate. They are the market data approach, the cost approach, and the income approach. Also, there are different levels within the above. For example, there is a short form appraisal sometimes called *"Summary"* or *"Limited."* I will discuss those after I review the three main approaches.

The Market Data Approach

In the market data approach, the appraiser identifies properties in the same market area that are similar to the subject property and compares the subject property to the comparable properties on the basis of lot size, use, etc. Positive or negative adjustments are made for differences in the features to arrive at an estimated value of the subject property.

The Process

The property that is being appraised is called the *"subject property"* and the other properties that are used for comparison are called *"comparable properties."* These comparable properties should be in the same market area. The comparables should have been sold recently and should be similar to the subject property in every possible way. The closer the comparable properties are to the subject property, the greater the similarity between the comparable and subject properties and the more recent the time of sale, the greater the accuracy of the appraised value.

It is preferred that there are at least three comparable properties used, but more can be used. Sometimes, it may be difficult to find three comparable properties that were actually sold. If the appraiser cannot find comparable sold properties they can use properties that are listed for sale. However, prices which properties are listed may not be the same as actual market prices. Remember, the properties have to be similar in use, such as office buildings compared to other office buildings. In many cases, there are different levels of quality of building, like luxury office space, with added features like a prestigious address, architectural design, on site food service available and quality of construction.

In performing the comparisons, the appraiser takes into account the location of the property, the site, view or location, the date of sale, financing concessions, and particular features of the properties.

To the extent that all the properties are in the same market area, it is not necessary to make an adjustment for the market area. However, if a comparable property is located in an area where prices are, generally higher, the price of the comparable property should be adjusted downward. Even if the properties are in the same market area, adjustments may be needed for differences in size, age and the other usual characteristics that make a property valuable.

Financing concessions can result in higher prices. When a borrower assumes a low-interest mortgage or when the seller finances the purchase at a rate lower than the going market rate, the purchaser would be willing to pay a higher price. In such cases, a downward adjustment is in order. A transaction between related parties may also require an adjustment. The price could be lower than the price in an arms-length transaction.

Finally, adjustments are made for differences in the features of the properties. Differences may include the quality of construction, age, condition, gross area, energy-efficient items, air conditioning, and the price of the comparable properties. The adjustments are rather subjective, and different appraisers can make different adjustments. As you can see, appraising realty is a science, but not as exact as one would expect or in some cases, like. With an experienced MAI appraiser, however, the adjustments will usually be the most accurate.

Advantages/ Disadvantages of the Market Data Approach

The main advantage of this approach is that it can generate fairly accurate indications of value when good comparables exist. It uses current market data. Furthermore, if good comparables exist, the data on the comparables can be obtained fairly easily. It is always easier to see the value differences when you have a long list of comparables. However, the market data approach would not work well if the comparables cannot be obtained or if the only comparables consist of properties on the market and extremely older sales.

The Cost Approach

For certain types of buildings, it may be difficult to find market data on comparable properties. Some examples are schools and sporting businesses, like bowling alleys. Church properties, unless they have an alternative use, are very difficult to find comparisons. For these and other similar buildings, the cost approach is better. The cost approach is used even for properties where comparables exist. Note, the cost approach is not very reliable unless the comparables are new. For fairly new buildings, the cost approach is appropriate. Should a lender need a newly constructed building appraised, the cost approach will work along with the other methods.

Using the cost approach, the appraised value is the cost of reproducing or replacing the property less accrued depreciation plus the value of the land. Reproduction cost means the cost of replicating the building using the same materials. If reproducing the property is not possible, the cost of an equivalent building is then used. This is called the *"replacement cost."*

The Process

The cost method involves the estimation of reproduction or replacement costs, reducing the costs by accrued depreciation and then adding the estimated value of land.

The first step is to estimate the total reproduction or replacement costs. There are three methods of estimating the reproduction or replacement costs. The first method is the *quantity survey method*, the second method is *the unit –in- place* method and the third method is the *comparative unit method*.

In the quantity survey method, the reproduction or replacement cost is estimated by adding the cost of labor and materials that would be needed to reproduce or replace the property. Items such as insurance are also included. While this method would be the most accurate, it is also the most expensive of the three methods mentioned above.

In the *unit-in-place* method, the total costs are based on the costs of the major components that have been installed. Examples of major components may include foundations, plumbing and roofing.

In the comparative method, replacement costs are based on unit costs of comparable buildings. Cost indexes are used in updating unit costs.

The next step is to estimate accrued depreciation. There are three types of depreciation. The first type of depreciation is physical deterioration. This type refers to any loss to the property value caused by normal wear and tear or usage. Also includes such things as termite damage and dry rot. The second type is the functional obsolescence of the property. This type refers to the decline in value or lack of desirability in terms of layout, style and design as compared with that of a new property serving the same function. The third type is economic obsolescence. This type refers to a loss in value from down turn in the market area, but outside the property itself.

Physical deterioration may or may not be curable. Curable items are those items that can be repaired. Incurable items are those that cannot be repaired at a cost smaller than the value added to the property by repairing the items.

Estimating accrued depreciation can be difficult. The easiest method of estimating depreciation, although not the most satisfactory is the straight -line method. Accrued depreciation is calculated as the product of the replacement cost and the ratio of the age of the building to the estimated life of the building. The major problems in this method are estimating the effective age and the economic life of the building.

The value of the land, assuming the land has not been improved, is estimated by using the market data approach.

Advantages/Disadvantages of the Cost Approach

The cost approach method is estimating the value of a piece of property by adding to it the estimated land value, the estimate of the replacement cost or reproduction cost of the building, less depreciation. Also called the *reproduction cost approach*. The cost approach method is the only way of estimating property when comparables are unavailable.

The disadvantage of the cost approach method is that it may not be able to produce a fair and accurate indication of value, especially if the property is an old property.

The Income Approach

The income approach method, more or less, is used to determine the value of the property by dividing net annual income by the capitalization rate. Also, this method can be called the capitalization approach method. The capitalization rate is a measure of the investor's profit. In real time, the income approach method is the estimation of the properties yearly net income and capitalizing the income using the appropriate rate of discount. In essence, yearly net income and net proceeds would be discounted to the present and the indicated value is established. Remember, the lender wants a safe investment, as does the borrower. Comparing the debt to the income can truly reveal the "real value" of the property. After all, the borrower pays the debt service from the NOI. The lender usually wants the borrower to not only be able to pay the debt, but make a profit of at least twenty to twenty-five percent of the NOI. Remember the debt service ratio?

The Process

I will begin with the formula for the *net operating income* or NOI. Below is the way to find the NOI.

Total Potential Income:
Less Vacancy rate= **Effective Gross Income**
Effective Gross Income:
Less-Expenses (Taxes, insurance & maintenance)
Less-Management fees
Total = Net Operating Income (NOI)

The simple explanation is the deduction of the expenses from the income. The operating expenses include such items as taxes, repairs and maintenance, management fees, telephone expenses, insurance premiums, legal and accounting fees, etc.

When the income property is appraised using the above formula, you have to understand that the income approach will require the owner or buyer to supply the records necessary to come to an opinion on the NOI. The usual records include the income tax returns and profit and loss statements. It also requires copies of any leases to determine the actual income and expenses. The appraiser will make a judgment as to what capitalization rate to use.

Besides the formula, is the need for the appraiser to make value judgments in areas that the record keeping may ignore. Many borrowers report that they have little, if any, maintenance costs on their property or they do it themselves and do not have the figures to show. Many appraisers see this as an effort to make the property look better or more valuable by not reporting maintenance or in fact, believe the borrower and have to come to a decision on the value of the maintenance. It is usually necessary for the appraiser to fill in a reasonable number to make sure that this area is covered.

One of the areas that the lenders and borrowers can disagree is the actual formulas used. The two areas that come into question are the management fees and the vacancy rate. Lenders look at the NOI as if the owner doesn't occupy the property and therefore even if the owner doesn't use a management company, it will use a reasonable figure, like 5%, as to reflect that a property management company is being used. Why do lenders believe it is necessary to have a built-in management rate? Should a default occur, the lender looks to the collateral. Upon default the lender takes possession of the property and now the lender would have to pay a management company fee. If the lender has to carry the foreclosed property while the property is for sale, it will be necessary to have a management company to preserve the asset or collateral.

Another area of expenses that is contentious is the vacancy rate expense deduction. To make a true comparison of all income properties, the rate of the vacancy allows the lender to see that even though a rental property or income property has a long and continual record of occupancy, it would not be unusual to experience some short periods, even a month or two in the course of a year or series of years. Even if there is a waiting list for an apartment building, there will be a transition period of vacancy of at least a month when one tenant leaves and another is brought in. The usual vacancy rate appraisers' use is 5% unless there is historical evidence that the appraiser can use to show why it should be higher or lower.

Now, when you divide the NOI by the sales price, you get the capitalization (Cap) rate. The lower the cap rate the better the property. For example, if the sales price is one million dollars and the NOI is one hundred thousand dollars, the cap rate is 10%.

The capitalization rate can also generate controversy. Investors believe that they need a certain rate. Sellers value their property using a certain rate to make the property seem more valuable and borrowers have their own agenda. Most appraisers try to find the market capitalization rate, which is explained by comparing other properties of like kind. It can be difficult. There are also sources of capitalization rates like The American Council of Life Insurance Companies. They examine properties and periodically announce capitalization rates on real estate.

With the difficulty of reaching a cap rate, many times the appraiser must strike a compromise. In some cases the appraiser leaves the actual cap rate up to the lender.

One more item under this topic is that the lender will take the loan terms and the income and develop the *"loan constant."* This allows the lender to compare the capitalization rate based on the NOI then subtract the debt service to determine the "true" yearly investment income. If you take the yearly NOI and deduct the debt service, you are left with the *"investment income"*. When you compare this to the purchase price you have the lender's own constant or the capitalization number.

Advantage/ Disadvantage of the Income Approach

As you can see there are many advantages to the first two methods of appraisal. However, as far as commercial and business properties, the income approach method is usually looked at by lenders as the most accurate means of judging the value of a property for lending purposes. It is extremely important for the lender to see the ability of the property to produce income to pay for the debt service. The fact that the property's income is used to pay for the debt service; it goes without saying lenders value the income approach method, usually above all other methods.

Another advantage of the income approach method is that it establishes the value using future income of the property. The disadvantage is estimating the net operating income and setting the capitalization rate can be a problem since there can be differing options and opinions on the capitalization rate. What all this yields is a mashing of teeth by all parties when they finally look at the appraisal and the income approach method.

Estimated Appraised Value

In many cases there are substantial differences when using all three methods. The appraiser will reach a value by giving more weight to the value generated by the most appropriate method for evaluating the property in question. Many commercial lenders will ask the appraiser to make sure they use all three methods but they value one method over the others. As stated, the income approach is usually the best or preferred method. The exception is in new construction loans.

Most lenders have, on staff, appraisers who review the outside appraiser's work. Many times the in-house appraiser will review the report and alter the outside appraiser's final value.

Also, there are many types of appraisals but most lenders use two different kinds of appraisals based on the amount of information included in the report. The two are summary or short form and the full appraisal or long form.

Many times, the lender is satisfied with a shorter version of the commercial appraisal and will allow the borrower's loan to be based on a summary appraisal. However, when the loan is large and riskier, the lender will usually want the most detailed and thorough report. One of the main differences between the two is the inspection of the property. The long-form will usually involve a detailed physical inspection of the interior, the exterior, the roof and HVAC systems and replacement costs for any repairs necessary. A short appraisal will usually work where the lender has previous knowledge of the property or the LTV is very favorable to the lender.

What does this all mean to a borrower? It means that one of the most important ingredients in the lending process is never as precise as all the parties would want. Highly debatable and at times frustrating, the borrower can be held hostage by a low appraisal. Too many times a seemingly good loan has been refused do to the lender not being comfortable with the appraiser's value of the property or the collateral. Many borrowers walk away confused and outraged by the fact that the lender's appraiser brought in a value so low that the LTV offered killed their loan.

Questions and answers on things you should know about appraisals

Q. Can a borrower dispute the lenders appraisal?
A. The borrower can dispute the lenders appraisal but must have clear evidence that the figures, income or comparables are wrong.
Q. Can a borrower hire their own appraiser?
A. A borrower can obtain their own appraisal but there aren't any guarantees that the lender will use it in granting a loan.
Q. Who owns the appraisal?
A. Even though the lender may pick the appraiser and the borrower pays the fees, the lender owns the appraisal, but the lender usually is obligated to give a copy to the borrower at closing or if they turn down the loan.
Q. Can another lender use an appraisal ordered by another lender?
A. Generally, the original lender must release the appraisal to the new lender. However, the new lender will ask the appraiser to certify the appraisal in the new lender's name.

Q. How long will an appraisal's value be used by a lender?
A. Usually, six months is the outside edge of the time limit. However, it is up to the lender. If the loan isn't closed within the six months, usually the lender will ask for an updated appraisal.

Noteworthy

- Remember, the commercial appraisal is more expensive than a residential appraisal and has to be paid for by the borrower before it is done.
- Have an accurate copy of all leases, income tax returns, and an income statement and expense statement prepared for the appraiser.
- While difficult to do, sometimes you can convince the lender to add value to an appraisal.
- Do not order your own appraisal then expect the lender to use it for the final decision on the value of your collateral.
- Usually appraisals over six months old are usually not reliable for most lenders.

CHAPTER 22
Mortgage Professionals & Business Brokers

Like all other professionals in the commercial lending process, the commercial mortgage professional, consultant or broker is a necessary ingredient to the majority of commercial borrowers. Like all the other issues over using an expert or professional, the experience and expertise of the borrower usually sets the tone as to whether a professional mortgage consultant or broker will be necessary. Many borrowers feel the additional fees paid to a broker are unnecessary. In addition, there are borrowers who need funding who have relationships with banks, which can help the borrower obtain a loan. This class of borrowers can make an appointment; bring in their information and walkout knowing more than likely the bank will do their deal. That situation is the exception to almost every rule, but it satisfies the old saying, "Banks only lend money to people who don't need it." However, for most borrowers, they do need a consultant or a broker to help them obtain a loan.

What is a Mortgage Broker?

When I decided to write this book, I spent time trying to set out some fundamental principles of commercial lending and to my amazement, there are few accepted principles and many debatable points of view. One key area is the use of mortgage brokers. Most people understand that a broker is a go-between or a person who arranges things. Therefore, the mortgage broker by definition arranges mortgages. However, there are over two- dozen recognized definitions from the simple one aforementioned, to a person who buys wholesale mortgages from lenders, then marks up the price and sells them.

What I did find is the consensus definition is: a mortgage consultant or broker is a trained professional with experience and the knowledge to find the right mortgage or funding for a client. The broker works for the client, for a fee, usually contingent on the client accepting the terms and is paid from the proceeds of the loan.

Many who have received a residential loan have done so by using a mortgage broker. Many residential brokers do commercial loans, but it usually pays for a borrower to hire a broker who only does commercial lending.

Commercial Loan Brokers

As I have stated, many residential loan brokers, on occasion, will lend assistance to a commercial client. The basic commercial loan broker who deals only with commercial funding is a specialists or an expert. This is not to diminish the residential loan broker. There are many residential brokers who are quite accomplished at placing commercial loans. It is to say that each has its own area and to be an expert in both can be very difficult. Obviously, if all you do is commercial lending or residential lending, you will be more qualified in your specific area. As I said in the legal area, you should hire a lawyer that does commercial or business work ahead of one that only does an occasional commercial deal.

There are other aspects of the commercial loan broker you should be familiar with. For example,

Broker's fees are usually from 1% to 3% and can be higher for the more difficult loans. Fees are charged and paid contingent on closing the loan. Many brokers charge an application fee to pay for expenses and the due diligence. The fees are usually based on the size and scope of the deal and many are not refundable. You should be careful about paying large upfront fees to a broker you do not know.

Other points to remember:

- Some lenders will pay the broker's fees, but most will not.
- Many brokers have special training from either working for lenders or have legal and accounting backgrounds.
- Brokers usually do not loan their own money.

- Many brokers help prepare a business plan as part of the broker's duties.
- Many brokers help the borrower during the settlement phase.

While some borrowers feel that paying a broker a fee may not be worth the employ, most do see the wisdom of bringing in an expert. The decision to employ a broker should be based on what the broker can accomplish for the borrower compared to what the borrower can do alone.

There are a number of questions to consider when you are debating whether or not to employ a broker.

- Do you feel that you know the industry well enough to go it alone?
- Will you involve your accountant or lawyer in your loan request?
- Will a broker make the difference in getting the loan? Will the broker will be able to get you the best terms?

Should you answers to the above questions be in the affirmative and decide to employ a broker, you should then be ready to ask the broker the following questions:

- Will the broker be doing the business plan?
- Has the broker placed your kind of loan before?
- How many lenders will the broker be working with and if a small number, why?
- What is the broker's confidence level for placing the loan?
- What is the fee arrangement?
- What percentage of work is commercial as opposed to residential lending?

Most borrowers don't ask any of the above questions and as a result they may not always be pleased with the broker. I have found that the best way to know the best broker is through a referral from someone who has worked with the broker or someone who you trust that knows a quality broker and can give you good advice.

Noteworthy

- A broker's services can be the difference between getting the best loan possible instead of accepting the first one offered.
- Make sure you understand the fee arrangement before hiring a broker.
- Hire the right broker for your loan request. Make sure the broker is an acknowledged commercial loan consultant or qualified mortgage broker.
- Only pay up-front fees when you are familiar with the broker and the history of work products.
- Make sure the broker you choose can help you with the business plan and other areas that you may need help.

CHAPTER 23
Environmental Reports

Another area of commercial lending that has produced much discussion and controversy is the commercial lender's concern over the environmental conditions on or around the realty and business used as the collateral for the loan. It is easy to see why a lender will not want to commit and close a loan where the real estate has significant environmental conditions that constitute a hazard to the environment or the enjoyment of the property as well as affecting the nearby property owners. Ground contamination by chemicals, petroleum products and hazardous waste has and will cause once valuable real estate to become valueless and not useable. Furthermore, many commercial parcels that are contaminated and yet the contamination goes undetected can require the owner to pay thousands and even millions of dollars in cleanup costs.

In order to combat the above possibilities, lenders demand inspections and make the borrower pay for them. If there are problems, the borrower can either choose not to take the loan or correct the problems to the lender's satisfaction.

If you are going to purchase or refinance commercial real estate, you should have at least a cursory understanding of the environmental inspections that a lender may require and an understanding of the experts that do the inspections.

Environmental Questionnaires

Many lenders, including most SBA lenders, try to determine the need for environmental inspection by having the seller or the owner of the property fill out an environmental questionnaire to determine what kind of inspection is necessary. The questions are obvious and the three or four page form basically asks for a history of the use of the property, asks for the kinds of storage tanks, if any, and other questions to try to narrow the specific type of inspection program that is needed. However, from my observations, almost all lenders request at least a Phase I or an ESA inspection.

Phase I Assessment (ESA)

Generally, the **ESA,** the *Environmental Site Assessment* or Phase I, is the initial inspection format where the lender has little or no knowledge of the property. In most cases, even with a questionnaire that doesn't reveal any signs of any contamination; the lender will still order an ESA inspection. The elements of the **ESA** are:

- A review of all available state and local government databases with information on the site. Any information available on storage tank removals or any permits to remove underground oil or gas tanks.
- A Building inspection, fire department and health department records check.
- A Federal database check.
- An interview with the current owners.
- A site inspection of the realty and the nearby properties.
- An evaluation of collected data to inform the lender of any risks and potential problems so the lender can make a decision as to whether or not to have further testing.

Phase II Assessment

Generally, the Phase II inspection is referred to as an *"intrusive assessment,"* since the inspection requires the inspectors to basically go into the ground or water supply. Usually, as a result of the Phase I report and any negative findings or recommendations, the lender asks for a Phase II. The following is a sample of the types of tests used:

- Monitoring of ground water and wells.
- Soil borings and testing.
- Underground storage tank testing.
- Asbestos inspections.

- Lead paint inspections.

Just as a Phase I inspection will result in a written report, the Phase II is a very detailed report of all testing done on the soil, water and other particles that are examined as a result of the recommendation by the Phase I report. This report is usually more detailed with scientific testing and the results thereto. At this point, the lender will make an assessment of what has to be done to "cleanup" or remediate the problems of contamination in accordance with the federal, state and local requirements. The most common problems are underground storage tanks that have by age developed leaks, ground water contamination from adjoining properties, buried hazardous waste, lead paint and asbestos particle problems.

It's obvious that costly environmental problems can cause a loan to fail. Site cleanup or remediation can be very expensive. Whether the loan is for an acquisition or a refinance, the borrower must understand that the environmental reports will be important and should plan for that expense.

Cost of Environmental Inspections

Unlike title insurance, where most states have regulations, environmental companies are not regulated. The result of no regulation is the price for the Phase I and especially the Phase II can vary from company to company and from state to state. Generally, the lender will choose the Phase I company and the fee will have to be paid by borrower prior to the inspection being done. Some lenders require the fee along with other due diligences fees, such as appraisals and others wait for the appraisals and other contingencies being met. This is why the questionnaire is important. Should the history of the property show a possibility of contamination, the lender will want the inspections or possibly any available old inspection reports or reports on any remediation measures completed.

Practical Tips

Especially, if the loan is a refinance, the borrower can do some positive things to either aid in the loan request or to save money. Make sure you keep copies of all prior inspections or environmental reports done by prior lenders. Many times, the company who performed the inspections still maintains a file and they will give you a better price for updating the report for the new lender.

If you know that your property has possible environmental problems, seek your own reports and pick a certified and reputable company at a competitive price. Many times, the lender will accept the report but don't always assume it. Also, if the property has a history of problems from the health department's inspections or the state or federal environmental agencies, make sure you have a copy. Also, make sure there aren't any issues open at the time of the loan request.

At the very minimum, do your own site inspection. If you see any possible problems, such as oil spots from a truck leaking oil or any improperly handled hazardous material, make sure you change or cleanup the area. Remember, if a Phase I company sees any signs of contamination, this can lead to a Phase II inspection, even though the problems are minor and easily remediated.

Environmental Insurance

In rare occasions some lenders request that the borrower buy an insurance policy that covers the lender if there are any environmental issues or claims. Like title insurance, the policy can cover the property owner. Rather than going through a long drawn out process of an evaluation of the environmental conditions, the lender and borrower can reach an agreement to have an insurance policy paid for from the borrower's funds usually at closing. Sometimes, in the case of an acquisition, the seller will contribute in order to get the deal done. Most policies are single payment, have deductibles and cover a set period of time.

The policies are used as follow:

- Streamline the due diligence process for real estate loans.
- Cost effective alternatives for borrowers not having to do a series of inspection due diligence.
- Can be used with the government's Brownfield Act. This allows sales of properties that are in the Super Fund Program. This pertains to any liability of a new property owner for any prior environmental cleanup problems.

This form of insurance can easily help the process. While not used in the general commercial lending networks, it can work well in the northeast states where there are commercial properties in environmental contaminated areas or located in fringe areas that have a long history of industrial contamination.

Noteworthy

- When anticipating an environmental inspection, make sure the property is clean, neat and free of any waste that could lead an environmental inspector to ask for a Phase II on the basis of surface particles or liquids.
- Keep all environmental records, old reports, etc.
- If the Phase I requests a Phase II, read the report for inaccuracies and challenge any errors.
- If you see an obvious environmental problem, deal with it prior to the loan request.
- Be prepared to pay an upfront fee from $750 to over $3,000 depending on the environmental history of the property.

CHAPTER 24
Title and Insurance

What is Title Insurance?

In most commercial loans, all or part of the loan requires some form of title insurance. Obviously, if the loan has real estate, the lender requires that a title company licensed by the state where the property is located insures the title and issues title insurance.

In almost all SBA guaranteed loans, the SBA and the lender will ask that the borrower offer additional collateral in the form of the borrower's personal residence. In that event, the title to that collateral is searched and insured. Remember, the lender requires a policy, but that policy insures only the lender. If the borrowers want coverage, this is done separately for additional costs paid for by the borrowers.

Why is it Necessary?

Many times a borrower questions the need for title insurance especially when the borrower has an existing policy and has controlled the property for many years. What you have to remember is that any title policy only covers incidents up to the issue of the policy. Also, many times the old policy may have been issued based on a search that may have been incomplete. The search may have missed items or that the prior title company failed to discover a problem that would now prevent a lender from closing a loan. I have found that even if a policy was issued, any prior mistakes by that company can hold up a closing. It can cost the borrower counsel fees and in some cases, the borrower misses a dead line that cost the borrower additional costs related to the lending process.

Where do you go for Title Insurance?

No matter whom you go to for title insurance be certain that the title company is licensed by the state where the property is located. Also, make sure that the company is approved by ALTA, which is The American Land Title Association. Founded in 1905, ALTA maintains the trade association of title companies.

Most commercial lenders require an ALTA *"marked up title"* or title search. In most states it is illegal for a lender to require a particular title company but the lender can specify the credentials of the company to make sure the company is appropriate.

Remember, most states mandate that the borrower can make the decision as to who does their title search. With that in mind the decision should be made carefully to insure that the title work is done in a timely manner with the borrower's interests at heart. Since most states regulate the maximum fee structure and maximum price for insurance, the fee is usually not a matter of shopping, although a careful borrower can get some concessions. Where a company recently did a title search you ask for a concession on price since the report merely needs up dating or bring-to-date information.

It's worth mentioning that a title company is not allowed to pay referral fees. When someone strenuously suggests a certain company, you should be aware that the relationship between that person and that title company may be too close and be sure you are making the right decision for the right reasons. However, if you do not know of a company, it pays to ask questions of the people you trust to recommend the name of a good company.

Part of the title search process is that the title company usually performs a judgment and lien search. As a buyer you are made aware of any money owed by the seller that must be accounted for at the closing. While the lender and lender's counsel will pay attention to this result of the search, you as a borrower should also make sure that nothing is missed.

If the loan involves a refinance, you should check with the title company to make sure that you do not have any outstanding issues that could hold up a closing. It is not uncommon for tax bills, and other items to appear as liens on a title search where they have been paid but not released. Situations like these can cause time delays and frustrations unless you deal with them in a timely fashion.

Another part of the title insurance phase of a commercial loan is the owner's policy. If the loan is for an acquisition of real estate, I always recommend that the borrower (buyer) gets the owner's policy. However, if the deal is for the refinance of realty, do not buy insurance since you may already have a policy and you continue as the owner. Make sure you look at the settlement sheet to make sure you are not being charged for owner's coverage. It is worth mentioning that the decision to buy owners coverage should be discussed with your attorney before a final decision.

Noteworthy

- Make sure you order a title search as soon as you receive a commitment where you feel the terms are such that the deal will close.
- Have your attorney review the title search information.
- Always buy title insurance on any acquisitions.
- Try to use a title company that you are familiar with or you know is competent.

CHAPTER 25
Realtors and Business Brokers

The two groups of professionals you may have significant contact with are realtors and business brokers. Realtors are licensed; they have a set of legal ethics and supposedly are trained to understand the sale of real estate. Some are very good and some not. The business broker is usually not licensed, although some are licensed realtors and they do handle transactions involved with the sale of businesses. They can either help you with financing, get in the way or as in most cases just handle the sales contract and do not interfere.

Realtor Issues

To begin with, many realtors realize that prior to the contract of sale and having an eye on the financing can help the deal to close. In addition, many times I have seen real estate contracts that are either overpriced, overvalued or are based on unsound principles. Many realtors do not understand that the more important part of commercial realty is the value placed on the income from the property as opposed to the value compared to other properties. As pointed out in the appraisal section, in order to properly value realty, you must put great importance on the actual income the property produces. As a borrower, you can help the realtor come to the right conclusion as to the income and the ability of that income to pay a certain debt service. You must remember, the loan to value is one main ingredient but the debt service ratio is more important since this gives the actual amount of money available for the payment of the loan. Too many times I have seen the offer to purchase completely neglect the actual income of the property. Understanding the commercial lending process can help you work with realtors.

Here are some positive things you can do to work with a realtor.

- Aid in the evaluation of the realty's income and expenses.
- Determine your viability to be financed based on the purchase price.
- Aide in drafting the offer to purchase.
- Help determine the closing date so that you have the necessary time to close.

Also, even though realty is the substantial asset, the proper drafting of the contract with *"other assets,"* like fixtures, equipment and liquor licenses can many times help a borrower receive funding. Many times there are conflicts between a buyer and seller over the breakdown of assets in a contract. The conflict usually arises do to tax issues. Understanding the issues and being able to compromise the confliction between the buyer and the seller can lead to a successful conclusion.

There are also many issues that can be a problem with working with realtors. I have found that too many realtors will invade the province of the commercial lending by giving incomplete or wrong advice about the financing to their client. Especially, the straight real estate transaction, many realtors who do primarily residential transactions will not understand the way commercial realty is financed and tell their clients the wrong estimated interest rates and terms. Also, many times realtors set an unreasonable closing date. I have seen closing dates set for as little as thirty days where it can take that long for a commercial appraisal, especially when the lender wants an MAI appraisal. Many realtors do not understand how difficult it can be to get funding, especially now with the banks becoming more conservative.

Here are some of the negatives when working with a realtor:

- Not analyzing the purchase price with an eye on getting the funding.
- Unrealistic dates in contract for a loan placement and the closing.
- The total lack of understanding of the differences between a residential deal and a commercial deal.

- The giving of wrong information to clients about the commercial lending process.

I don't want you to think that the above is the average realtor. I have found that the great majority of realtors who sell commercial realty do understand the overall process and can be an asset in the lending process. However, it is also clear that many realtors who do not specialize in commercial realty do not. You must be ready to deal with the negatives, as well as the positives.

Business Brokers

Many of the above positives and negatives apply to the business broker. Just to make sure you understand the business broker generally is involved with <u>non-realty</u> based business assets and contracts. For example, the pizza restaurant in the shopping mall. The purchase contracts will be different, the lenders many times different and the terms surely different. To be successful in working with the business broker is practically the same as with a realtor. If the business broker represents you as a buyer and you are going to borrow money, makes sure the business broker understands the process of getting the funding. Likewise, the negatives are almost the same as working with a realtor. Also, like realtors, most professional business brokers are generally versed in the commercial lending process and can help.

Noteworthy

- Do not allow the realtor or business broker to control the lending terms.
- Try to work with the realtor or business broker on your financing contingency before the contract is signed.
- Do not blindly accept a realtor or business broker's advice on financing.
- Make sure you completely understand the financing available before you sign a contract.

- Remember that the realtor and business broker's first concern is to get the deal closed and is not as concerned with you getting the best lending terms available.

PART FIVE
OTHER IMPORTANT ITEMS

CHAPTER 26
Credit Scoring

The term "fico" score was named after the Fair Isaac Company that designed the computer software that is used by the credit reporting agencies.

What is credit scoring?

Controversial, but necessary, credit scoring is the system used by lenders to aid them in their decision whether a borrower deserves to be granted credit or given a loan. Also, other industries are using the information for their decision-making, like landlords, life insurance companies and car insurance companies.

Most lenders use the *FICO* or credit score of a borrower to either eliminate or allow a borrower to move towards being considered for a loan. While not being the only consideration, many lenders set an arbitrary level where if the borrower is below that mark, the borrower is automatically eliminated for consideration. While this position isn't always fair, it is a situation that you as a borrower have to deal with if you are seeking a loan.

Using the collection of specific statistical data, the credit agencies assemble a profile, which is reflected in the *FICO* or credit score.

The data used to form the score is separated into five specific areas.

- Payment history.
- Types of credit.
- Amounts owed.
- Length of credit history.
- Number of new credit or inquires.

How does payment history affect a score?

This category may be the most important. Over 35% of your total score comes from this category. There are a number of factors that go into your payment history.

- Number of past due items and severity of each.
- Number of accounts paid on time.
- Adverse public records showing past due items, like bankruptcy and judgments.
- Time since delinquencies on record.
- Collection amounts due.
- Total amount of collection items.

As you can see, the payment history is very important and is the category that contains the most information.

How amounts owed effect credit?

Obviously, the amounts owed give an indication of the credit worthiness. This category accounts for 30% of the score. The following items are part of this category:

- Amounts owed on your accounts.
- Total amount owed on all accounts.
- The number of accounts with open balances.
- Proportion of credit used to the total credit limit

How does the length of credit history affect score?

Your credit history and the length of your credit are important and amounts to 15% of your score. The important factors of this item are:

- Time since accounts opened.
- Time since account active.
- Time since opened on specific accounts.

What types of credit used effects score?

Another part of the score, worth 10%, is based on the types of accounts and the type of credit. It goes without saying that if the credit is all credit cards, that the score will be affected. This category looks to the various types of credit used.

Does new credit affect the score?

A smaller part of the score, 10%, is devoted to looking at new credit. The following represents the items looked at in this category.

- Number of recent credit inquires.
- Time since credit inquires.
- Number of recently opened accounts.
- Time since re-establishing the credit.

Does the number of inquiries affect the score?

The credit scoring companies do use as a negative, the amount of inquires made against the credit account. Obviously, an unusual amount of inquires indicate that a borrower is possibly having a difficult time obtaining a loan.

For example, I was working with a real estate builder-developer who was heavily leveraged because of the real estate slowdown of the late months of 2007. When I pulled his credit there was over 90 credit inquires in a six-month period. Needless to say, the client was in deep trouble.

It goes without saying if you can limit the inquires, it will help you. This is extremely important where the borrower's credit is on the lower end of the credit-scoring target of above 600, average score.

Is a personal score important for a commercial loan?

While no doubt exists that credit scores are an important consideration by a lender. However, in many cases you may be surprised that it isn't the most important. Usually, the credit score is just one of the many factors that a lender uses in making a lending decision. However, the importance of the score relates to the kind of loan the borrower is trying to obtain. It is considered along with the other relevant information. Also, in many loans for commercial property or business financing, there are commercial credit scores on the business you are acquiring or on refinancing the real estate. In the next chapter, I will discuss the commercial credit system.

Unlike residential lending, where the score is extremely important, the commercial lender usually has many other important considerations, like the quality of the collateral, the income of the business assets pledged and the resume of the borrower.

One type of commercial loan that the credit is a main factor is asset based commercial real estate loans where the credit and the loan-to-value are the basic considerations.

Noteworthy

- Bad credit can kill the chances for a commercial loan, but good credit doesn't necessarily get you a loan.
- Many lenders set an arbitrary minimum credit score at the 550 to 600 FICO score as the baseline before considering a loan.
- Since the number of inquiries on the credit account can lower the score, make sure that there are limited inquires. Do not send your loan to an unreasonable amount of lenders.
- Before asking for a loan, make sure you know your FICO score. If you have late payment items, have your explanations ready. If you have had a bankruptcy, explain the reason and do go into detail on how the creditors were affected. What was the value of all claims excused in the bankruptcy?
- Do not hesitate to challenge mistakes on your credit report. Make a timely request to correct any mistakes.
- If you feel you need professional help with getting your credit straightened out, make sure that the company you choose is competent and the fees are reasonable.

CHAPTER 27
Small Business Credit

As previously stated, a small business, most of the time, is judged by the credit score of the principles, owners, partners or guarantors. It is difficult to separate the personal credit of the owners from the business credit. Since most lenders will always check the personal credit of all the principals, it becomes paramount for all borrowers to know and be aware of the all personal credit. It can help if the small business owner does more to show how the business can perform from a credit standpoint.

What can a small business do to help itself? The first thing that can be done is to make sure that any credit for the company or business is in fact in the company's name, regardless of whether the owner is a guarantor. Many small companies buy equipment, vehicles and items for commercial use on credit in the owner's name. If possible, have all the company credit in the actual name of company so the various credit organizations can follow the credit history.

Another way to help the credit of a small business is to cooperate with the credit reporting agencies, like Dunn and Bradstreet. Known as D & B, this company is the pillar of the commercial credit reporting system. Cooperating with reporting agencies means that they can have your company listed and have the company's credit history available for lenders and vendors. Too many times, an inquiry is made on a new business causing Dunn & Bradstreet to ask the company for information or the guarantors for information and they either refuse or simply do not respond to the information request.

The Paydex System

Probably one of the more important credit organizations is the Paydex agency of the Dunn and Bradstreet credit reporting company. The Paydex system is the ranking system that marks the ability of a business to pay its bills in a timely fashion using the total number of payment experiences in the D & B files. The scores are rated from 0 to 100. For example, if the score is 50 to 79, this means a medium risk or the company or business is average in paying its bills. If the company has a score below 50, the lender can take away from that score that probably the company is a high risk for a loan because of a history of late payments, meaning beyond 120 days.

Now, if you are contemplating a business loan in the name of your company, you should immediately find out you Paydex score. Like the personal credit scoring talked about in previous chapter, you should make sure that the score is correct. You should periodically check the Paydex score and if there is a problem, make sure it is corrected. While not as complex or as complicated as the FICO scores, the Paydex score can be the difference between getting a loan or being turned down. Likewise, there are other credit organizations and it pays to make sure they all have the correct information.

Noteworthy

- Try to have credit established in the company or business name as soon as possible.
- Try to have personal guarantees removed from company credit as soon as possible.
- Cooperate with all commercial credit-reporting agencies, especially D & B or their affiliate companies.
- Maintain your Paydex score as close to 80 as possible.
- Constantly monitor all credit reporting agencies. repo

CHAPTER 28
Construction Loans

Far and apart from other types of commercial loans, is the basic construction loan. This type of loan or financing occupies a special place.

Normally, the lender will analyze the building, the business and the borrowers before making the lending decision. However, with construction financing there are other considerations. There are many more details for the lender to review before being comfortable with a construction loan request.

First and foremost, the lender will need the usual and customary information on the borrower and the business as set forth previously. With a construction loan, the actual construction details are examined by the lender's own construction experts. Too many times, construction loans fail because the borrower's information is incomplete. For example, some borrowers do not have the funds to give the lender a complete set of drawings and a final site plan. Remember, architectural drawings and engineering drawings can be very expensive. It can be very expensive to prepare a construction loan request. Since the amount of necessary information for a construction loan package can cost thousands of dollars, the borrower should use caution before attempting the project. Too many times I have seen naïve real estate investors embark on a project where after spending a large amount of money on zoning approvals and site plan approvals the investor is forced to sell the project because the investor's low liquidity prevents the borrower from moving forward with a commercial loan.

As a borrower, once you are convinced that a sound decision has been made for a construction project, you will have to prepare for the lender the following information:

- A detailed description of the project, including all drawings or plans.
- The background and resumes of the architect, the engineer and the contractor. They should contain as much information as possible on their individual qualifications, past projects, etc.
- A line item breakdown of costs supplied by the estimates from all contractors.
- The contractor's draw schedule.
- The survey or plat of the property.
- All engineering studies and site plans with copies of all approvals.
- All environmental reports.
- Profit and loss projections on the building.
- Market information on the rentals that compare with your building

Obviously, the borrower has to show that the construction will result in a building or buildings that will have an appraised value whereby the loan-to-value will be within the limits of the lender's requirement set out in the loan commitment. Remember, the initial loan commitment, like all others, will require an appraisal of the building that is to be constructed. You must be able to give the appraiser as much information as possible in order that the appraiser can give an accurate value. The more complete the information the better the appraisal will reflect the true future value. Commonly called a *"as built"* or *"as completed appraisal,"* this contingency in the loan commitment can be the item that makes or breaks the loan request.

There are problem areas that can confront a borrower in a construction loan. If the site plan has not been approved, lenders will not close the loan. Make sure that before you accept terms of loan that you have the proper zoning and site plan approval, otherwise you are wasting everyone's time. Most lenders, including all SBA loans, require a performance bond from the contractor. Also, it can be difficult for a borrower to do their own construction unless the borrower is a licensed contractor. Critical to the loan request is the borrower arriving at the bottom line construction costs. Remember, the costs are estimates, so provide an additional 5% contingency above the completed cost estimates. Anytime a borrower must use estimated expenses or costs, it can cause a lender to move slowly or to reject the loan merely because the borrower has not presented the loan with clearly proper factual support of the final costs of construction.

Also, like all commercial loans, lenders will want environmental reports and may require soil testing. Another requirement will be reports from utility companies and the local government agencies specifying that water services, sewage connections, electric power and telephone services will be provided to the property. Make sure that the lender's draw schedule is reasonable for the contractor to get the funding at the correct times.

As you can see, to put together a viable construction loan request, the borrower will have to include much more details and information than is usually included. The organization of all the details necessary in order to impress the lender can be a difficult chore for anyone. Should the lending package be incomplete leaving the lender confused and repeatedly asking questions, the lender will usually turn down the loan request. I always recommend that an inexperienced borrower, hire a qualified professional to help secure a construction loan.

Noteworthy

- Do not submit a construction loan without having all of the necessary items, especially the costs.
- Make sure you have all zoning approvals and site plan approvals <u>before</u> submitting loan.
- Make sure you have a resume from the contractor, architect and engineer available for the lender to review with the loan request.
- Always provide at least a 5% reserve in the loan amount for any miscellaneous, additional items and expenses.
- Remember, construction funding usually needs the expert help from either an accountant or mortgage broker who knows the construction lending arena.

CHAPTER 29
Start Up Business Loans

Just like construction loans, the start-up business loan occupies another special place in the commercial lending process. By far the most difficult type of loan, it takes real know-how to put together a successful start-up loan package. Most of the difficulty comes from the need for the lender to feel comfortable with the financial projections showing the potential profits.

As stated earlier, where most lenders rely on historical numbers from a business, usually from tax returns, the lender who is contemplating granting a start-up loan, must look elsewhere to gain confidence in approving a startup loan. In almost every start-up, the lender is faced with making a tough decision based on the future of a business project rather than basing the decision on the past production of income. Because of the difficulty, the borrower has additional pressure to explain the loan request.

To begin with, the borrower should follow the usual loan request procedures as outlined in Chapter 3. You must start with the organization of financial information and review of credit. Where the loan request becomes more difficult is at the business plan stage and doing a start-up plan.

Start-up Business Plan

To begin with, the business plan is crucial in a business loan. I have always felt that the ability to convince the lender of the credit worthiness of the business borrower begins and ends with proving that the loan can be paid back from the proceeds of the business. It sounds so simple. However, with a start-up loan, the job of proving the worth of the business means that the borrower has two prongs to satisfy. Since it is a startup, everything is looked at under a microscope.

First, the lender has to know, in great detail, all the qualifications of the borrower to operate the income producing business and in particular, the business that will be making the debt payments to the lender.

Secondly, the lender has to be satisfied that all of the right information on the business is included in the business plan. What this means is that the business plan must contain such information that the lender is satisfied that every question has been answered to the lender's satisfaction.

To begin with, have the business plan outline done to the point of having the crucial financial numbers in place. The key will be with a start-up, to prove how you arrived at the financial projections. It will be necessary to show that you have sourced the business plan with research, possibly other business statistics or business numbers from a business that the borrower has previously worked in or owned. Here is the catch. The borrower's personal background, education and experience will give the lender comfort with the loan. How does that work?

If you are a lender and you are reviewing a business plan whereby the borrower has statistical back up of the various points in the plan and the borrower has worked with the same type of business, the chances are good that the lender will feel comfortable with the loan.

Start-up Summary

What must be included in the business plan that sets the tone is the *start-up summary*. Here the borrower sets out, in detail, how the proceeds of the loan will be particularly used to get the business up and running.

Below is a sample of what goes into a start-up summary. This is for a start-up pizza delivery business without real estate. Assume the business is leasing a storefront. You must itemize the following:

- The legal costs for formation of the business and following through with the loan request, including the closing.
- The costs of the *build-out* (renovations) of premises to install a pizza kitchen.
- The costs of kitchen and operating equipment both new and used.
- Cost of the opening inventory, such as paper products, food products and other products necessary to open and for at least the first three months.
- All insurance costs for the first year.
- The costs of signs as well as opening advertising.
- Rent for three months.
- Utility costs for three months.
- The amounts of deposits necessary for starting up the business.
- Three months of debt service.
- An amount for miscellaneous expenses based on a small percentage of overall costs, like a 5% contingency.

When the above is complete, the lender will know that you have the exact amount of funds necessary to open and run the business for three months or the time necessary to bring the business to a profit. The lender will understand that you know what is actually needed. Also, you can see many of the items, such as the money to pay the debt service, etc. will be in the form of working capital. Without working capital, a small business start-up would not work, nor does a lender give a borrower a loan.

When you have the total necessary funds set out, you can then show the lender what capital you will inject so a reasonable loan amount can be set.

In order to put this plan into focus, please note below the contents necessary for the start-up business plan. Like all business plans, the startup plan must show in as much detail as possible the way the borrower will run the business for a profit. The difference is the startup plan will have no historical facts to back up the projections of income and expenses. Make sure your plan contains the following:

1. Executive Summary
   a. Objectives
   b. Mission
   c. Keys to Success
2. Company Summary
   a. Start-up Summary
   b. Company Ownership
   c. Company Location and Facilities
3. Products
4. Market Study
5. Competition
6. Sales Strategy
7. Management Plan/ Personnel Plan
8. Financial Plan
   a. Break-even Analysis
   b. Projections of Profit and Loss
   c. Projected Balance sheet

As previously stated, with the resumes of the borrowers, the management resumes become magnified when looking at the business plan of a start-up. The bottom line of the plan is will the lender be satisfied that the borrowers have the skills, knowledge and understanding to carry out the plan? Also, did the borrowers substantiate with facts that the financial projections are reasonable and workable in the industry or business enterprise of the borrower? Unsupported projections can only lead to a turndown. Even supported projections by the borrowers with little or no background or resumes may also lead to a turndown. As hard as it is to start-up a new business, the success of the venture primarily falls on the borrower's abilities combined with the right amount of capital either through equity investment or debt in the form of business loans.

Later, I will show you how all of the above comes together in a start-up SBA loan for a restaurant. Remember, restaurant startup financing is very difficult.

Noteworthy

- The startup business plan has to be supported by substantial factual support.

- Make sure that loan amount accounts for enough funding to insure success of the business plan.
- Be prepared to provide evidence of the borrower's capital injection.
- Makes sure you provide the lender with the resume and qualifications of the borrower.
- Remember the key to a startup loan approval is making sure that the lender is satisfied that the borrower has proven that the projected income

will be able to pay the debt service.

CHAPTER 30
Financing a Franchise

In modern America, the influence of franchises is everywhere from car repairs to restaurants. Many franchises are the key to small business ownership. Some are extremely expensive, but many are within the grasp of many people with entrepreneurial dreams.

Since many books have been written on the subject of picking and buying a franchise I will just caution anyone considering buying a franchise, read everything you can and read everything three times. You should be aware of the consequences of your decision. Many times I have come across people who have bought franchises and found themselves almost a captive of that company having little control over their own business.

So, let's decide that we have found a franchise. How do we finance the purchase, either from the franchisor or from a franchisee?

Like buying any business, you begin with marshaling your own capital, checking your credit and organizing your financial records. Where a difference occurs in this process is at the business plan stage. Since you are buying a business that has its own basic business plan, including a set program for sales, profits and expenses, you have a leg up on most business purchases. However, you will have added expenses to pay as a result of your purchasing a franchise.

If you purchase a business directly from the franchise, you must account for the franchise fee, the training format, which includes training the owners and in many cases, the manager. You may also have to pay for other expenses which can include paying for franchise personnel who assist in finding a location and helping you with the build out or purchase of the location.

But, you will also get additional help with your financing. Here are some of the positives:

- Lenders are usually familiar with your franchise and will accept the profit and loss projections easier than with a non-franchise location.
- Many franchises offer help with financing.
- Most lenders feel more comfortable with a borrower that has gone through the pre-screening process that most franchises require before approving a buyer.
- Lenders also feel more comfortable with a borrower who will go through the training program offered by the franchise.
- Lenders realize that the franchise will want the buyer to succeed and will give the buyer assistance and in many cases negotiate the sale of a franchise where the buyer has not been successful.

When a borrower is buying a franchise from a franchise seller or owner, as opposed to buying directly from franchisor, in many cases the fact that the business entity is part of a network of other identical business entities, can help the borrower get funding. There are exceptions to this rule. Where a franchise location has not been successful over a reasonable period of time, a lender may not have comfort with a new owner, unless a clearly definable reason can be shown for the failure of the franchise and a clearly definable cure can be offered by the new owner. For example, if the franchise is a restaurant and it is located in area that has not been successful, a new owner usually cannot make any significant changes, since the business is restrictive on product, on price and method of operation. With a non-franchise location, the new owner can offer a menu change, a price and quality change.

Overall, funding of a franchise can come from the usual sources, depending on the amount of cash injection. If you have 25% or more, conventional banks usually will do a recognized franchise. If you don't have that much cash, the SBA or local governmental loan programs can be of great help. Remember, in most government-assisted loans or guarantees, the cash investment are usually at least 10%. When you combine the SBA and related lending sources to the tried and true franchises, it can be a little easier to become your own boss.

SBA FRANCHISE REGISTRY

As a matter of general information the SBA has established a registry for franchises that are approved for SBA financing. Anyone who ever applied for a loan for a franchise understands that essential to the process is the lender's review of the legal relationship established between the franchise and the buyer. The foundation of the relationship between the franchisor and franchisee is the franchise agreement. Besides the agreements, not unlike other business loan acquisitions the lender also reviews the strength and weaknesses of the franchise to determine if the deal is worth financing. The SBA registry makes this job so much easier.

Owing to the complexities as stated above, the SBA in the early nineties began a registry to approve not only the particular franchises for financing but to make sure that the legal arrangements that went with the franchises were fair and equitable to the buyer of the franchise and to the greater point protected the lender from loaning money to a franchise and at default finding out that the franchise agreement is an obstacle for the protection of the lender and franchisee.

What the SBA put in place is a registry that qualifies franchises for financing where any lender can use the registry to decide whether to grant a loan to a borrower who is buying a franchise. Now, not only does the registry approve franchises, but it keeps up on any material changes to the franchises and the franchise agreements to insure the continued approval of the franchise on the registry.

If you ever tried to read the franchise agreements and interpret them for your client, you will thank the SBA for its registry.

As a borrower who wants to invest in a franchise, the first place you look is at the SBA Franchise Registry. This is not to say that if you do not find your particular franchise approved that you should not follow through with the deal. You must understand that not all the franchises that do not qualify for the registry are somehow not worth buying. Many small franchises do not qualify since they do not have the size, the amount of minimal time required or the franchise has not even tried to qualify. Understand it is the franchise who takes it upon itself to submit to the standards of the registry.

However, it has been shown that the default rate for franchises on the registry is less than the default rate for those who are not and usually even better than the default rate for all businesses. Take my word that you must check the registry before even asking for a loan for a franchise whether you are using an SBA loan product or any other type of financing.

To further illustrate the importance of the registry, the following is what you learn by using the registry.

- The registry shows what franchises meet the technical requirements for an SBA loan.
- The registry makes the process of financing more efficient and facilitates the review of the franchise and the franchise agreements.
- The registry lowers the risk for the lender and thus the borrower.
- The registry provides lenders with a BCR or Bank Credit Report, which again ascertains the risk.
- The registry is a good source of information to decide whether a buyer-borrower wants to seriously move forward with a franchise
- The use of the registry is a good place to compare the different franchises
- Almost all lenders whether SBA or not will use the registry to decide whether to make a loan.

As you can see, the SBA Franchisee Registry is a great tool for the average borrower who wants to buy and finance a franchise.

Noteworthy

- Make sure your franchise can be financed before committing or signing an agreement with a franchise
- Check with the franchisor for help with lending sources. Many times, a particular lender has a portfolio of loans from one particular franchise.
- Check with other franchisees as to where they received their funding.
- Be extremely careful when buying a franchise location that has not been successful.
- If you are buying a successful franchise, go to the bank or lender that started-up that franchise location for help with the transaction.
- Make sure you are aware of all the additional charges and fees that come with buying a franchise before committing to a purchase.
- Be sure that you are familiar with all the regulations and rules of the franchise and whether they will be a hindrance to your particular way of operating a business entity. Are the rules too restrictive?
- Always check with the SBA Franchise Registry before making any decisions on buying a franchise or a franchise unit from a private party.
- Remember that not all franchises are on the registry and the fact that they are not does not disqualify them for purchase or financing.

CHAPTER 31
Real Estate Investment Lending

Apart from owner-occupied lending where the borrower actually operates a business out of the realty location is the real estate investment borrower. As is the case with most commercial banks and lenders, they view the two kinds of loans differently. While the general commercial lending rules apply, the lender when looking at the investor loan will consider other factors normally not given as much substance in owner-occupied loans requests. It is extremely important for you to understand the way the lender looks at investor income producing properties and investor loans.

The Borrower

Let's start with the investor borrower and the borrower's qualifications. Generally speaking owning investment properties is not for everyone. Many people believe that owning income producing property is an easy task. There are many who go into investing in real estate that are naïve and end up losing money. Likewise, the shrewd and intelligent investor can do very well. Some of America's great fortunes had begun with income producing real estate. Lenders know this. A real estate investor should have the following qualifications:

- A higher general financial liquidity above that required by the owner-occupied borrower. Remember, unlike an owner occupied property where the owner has a business profit, the investor property has to stand on the rental income.
- Real estate management skills whereby the borrower can demonstrate that they can effectively manage lease and maintain commercial real estate.

- Background and training commensurate with the size and complexity of the real estate investment.
- A demonstration of the overall understanding and judgment of being a real estate investor.

Not to over complicate the process, it is easily seen that a lender will look at the borrower closely to make sure that the real estate investment will be properly managed. Should your loan be for a single family residence to be used for a rental, the borrower's liquidity, management and business skills do not have to be as much an issue as with a 100 unit apartment complex.

The liquidity issue will always be a paramount consideration with investor financing. As previously stated, liquidity is the borrower's ability to have the cash available to handle a problem either in a business or investment. With owner-occupied properties, there are two entities that can provide liquidity, the borrower and the business owned by borrower. With the investment property there is only one source, the borrower.

Management and the ability to market, lease, and maintain a property is clearly important. Again, the size and scope of the property is an issue. A borrower with little experience or training in real estate management or business management may have a difficult time obtaining a loan for a larger project but not for a smaller project. Even though larger projects can have the income to afford a management company, the borrower still has to be able to show an ability to be a good, responsible business person. This is usually shown with experience and education.

The Property/ Investment

One of the essentials of financing income producing property or investment property is justifying the purchase price and establishing the net rental income and the net operating income or NOI. Your client must remember that the lender looks differently at the profit and loss statement. Most owners of real estate that produces an income will give you the net income based on the actual expenses deducted from the actual income. This may be the reality of owning the property, but commercial lenders look at the net income from their own perspective. Now, the lender will want a comprehensive rent roll which will highlight each unit, the rental amount, the name of tenant, whether the lease is in writing and what expenses are paid by the tenant. From this, the lender will be able to judge the profit and loss statements. Generally, most small buildings on the market will come with a set of profit and loss figures like the following:

Rental units: 6 apartments

History of occupancy: 100% for last two years

Tenants Pay: All utilities

Total rental income: $130,000

Purchase Price: $750,000

Now, the seller showed your borrower the following yearly expenses:

Electricity for common areas:	$1,200
Water/ Sewer expenses:	4,800
Insurance:	8,500
Pest Control:	300
Repairs: (actual)	3,121
Taxes:	6, 545
Misc.	500
Total:	$24, 966

Net Operating Income: $105,034

Obviously, this looks like a terrific deal for the buyer. If the buyer can pay cash, the buyer has a great income. However, this buyer wants to put down $150,000 and finance $600,000.

Now here is what the lender looks at when figuring the NOI. The lender will take the gross rents and deduct a 5% vacancy rate or $6,500, leaving an adjusted gross rent of $123,500.00. A common question is if the seller shows 100% occupancy, why then the deduction of 5% for vacancy? Obviously, no matter how good the property there will be a vacancy now and then, if only for a month, ready the unit for a new tenant. The lender believes that a 5% figure is proper. Now, if the property lies in an area where the vacancy rate on average is above 5%, many times the rate will reflect the local average. From the adjusted gross, the lender deducts the expenses as set forth from the seller except as to maintenance. The lender will take 5% of the income, or $6,175 for their maintenance figure deduction. They will add an additional expense of 5% for management fees. Why would the lender deduct a management fee if the borrower tells the lender that they will manage the property? The answer is the lender upon the default of the borrowers will have to carry the property until the property is sold and therefore they want the protection of the 5% maintenance and the 5% management fees.

So, the following are the expenses used by the lender to determine the NOI:

Electricity for common areas:	$1,200
Water/ Sewer expenses:	4,800
Insurance:	8,500
Repairs%	6,175
Taxes:	6, 545
Management fee: 5%	6,175
Misc.	500
Total:	$33,895
Net Operating Income:	$89,605

As you can see there is a difference. Is that difference enough for your buyer/ borrower to back off the deal? I would think not.

Now, based on the net income, how much will the lender loan the buyer? The lender will want at least a 1.25 debt ratio meaning for every dollar of income, the lender will allow for debt service of .75 cents. In this case the maximum allowed would be $67,203 or 75% of NOI. If the bank offers $600,000 loan at 7% for 20 years, the debt service would be $55,821. Obviously, the lender is satisfied with the *debt service ratio*.

Since the borrower is putting down 20% of purchase price or $150,000, then more or less, the lender would make the loan. This of course would be if the borrower is liquid, has at least some experience in ownership of income properties and has good credit. This all would be evaluated with the loan request and the management plan offered by the borrower. You as the borrower would be concerned with preparing the management plan and loan request. Do not forget that there will be closing costs in addition to the cash injection of $150,000.

To be an informed borrower you must know the difference between the seller's numbers and the lender's bottom line NOI. Rarely, the seller or the realtors will ever give you the figures that the lender's use to determine the NOI. What this leads to is the profit figures presented from the seller and then the profit as figured by the lender.

When I stated earlier the commercial lending rules many times prevents a buyer/borrower from making a bad business deal, this system of evaluation clearly represents that principle.

Noteworthy

- Your due diligence on investor loans is much greater on the collateral than owner-occupied.
- Make sure you understand the lender's NOI, along with the loan-to-value of the income producing real estate collateral.
- Do not forget that all of the usual rules of commercial lending apply, like doing a management plan, rent roll and submit copies of any leases as well as financials.

- If an acquisition try to verify the amount of repairs that are charged off on the owner's expense sheet and try to estimate what a new owner will have to pay since many small investor properties are owned by people who do their own repairs.

CHAPTER 32
Sources Not Recommended

When I sat down to write this book, I wanted to present a simple orderly discussion of small business and real estate lending for the entrepreneur or investor. What I didn't want to do was to stray from traditional commercial lending. Over the years I have read many books, articles and also listened to presentations by respected professionals listing many unconventional sources of capital for realty and small businesses. In almost every situation, I have reminded myself that when a borrower removes all the safeguards of rational traditional lending, the borrower may jeopardize not only future success but can lose all that the borrower has worked for over the years. While I do not recommend the following sources of capital, I will set out briefly those areas that a determined or maybe even a desperate borrower can turn to for money.

Borrowing from a 401(k) plan.

In earlier chapters, I spoke of *"hard money"* loans and repercussions of those loans where the borrower takes the funding but doesn't have a real good plan for an exit out of the loan. I feel the same when a borrower considers a loan from their retirement plan.

On its face, the thought of borrowing money from a retirement plan really doesn't seem like such a bad idea. After all, the money belongs to the borrower and the fact that the borrower is using the money to start a business or to help the borrower along seems like a good idea. However, there are many pitfalls along the road to borrowing from a retirement plan.

Essentially, what you are doing is to establish a plan that will allow the money from your 401 (k) to be transferred to a plan that can loan the money without the IRS taking a 20% penalty. You will have to have an attorney, an accountant, an expert in evaluation of stock and a stock brokerage house to handle the transaction.

So, you can see the first problem, fees. The second problem I see is that if you are not able to raise money with the use of conventional or traditional sources, maybe the deal is not worth the risk. But, my third problem is the 401 (k) plan is the safety net by which a person or family can rely on when the income years are up. In my judgment, only the few who are so talented and smart should even attempt this type of funding.

I know that many veterans of corporate America have left the fold to begin their own ventures this way, but again I say only the most experienced and smartest should use this method. There are many publications that can be found that will give you an idea of the ramifications of this process. For me, I would think it through and if you still feel you want to proceed, think about it some more. If anything, hire the right expert to evaluate what you are doing. Again, be safe and secure with your business plan as well as your plan transaction.

Credit Card Factoring

Let's face it, sometimes a business is in need of a quick infusion of capital to either stimulate the business activity, pay off unexpected debt or emergency funds for other necessary purposes. With no collateral or with the need to get cash fast, the use of credit card receipts can be a source.

Obviously, this form of lending is where the borrower or company has a credit card system in place for their customers. The *factoring* of credit card receivables consists of the borrower giving up a portion of the business's credit card receivables for a cash payment. By doing this, the lender collects the borrower's credit card receipts, takes out their share and applies same against the debt owed. Sounds simple, but what is the catch? You probably guessed it. It's the rate and terms.

To be honest, this method of getting fast capital can work for the benefit of the borrower if the amount of capital is absolutely necessary; it is for a short term with a guaranteed exit plan for payoff.

If all of these factors are there, it can work. If any are missing, I do not recommend.

The basic lending process is the following:

- Fill out application which includes the initial facts about the borrower and company.
- Submit proof of credit card business along with the credit card service statements and bank statements.
- The lender will gauge the loan on the history of credit card use, the amount of credit card receipts and of course the credit worthiness of the borrowing entity.
- As a borrower be prepared for the following: the lender will want to have full control of all credit card processing, the lender usually will charge more processing fees, and the lender will charge a larger interest rate and a shorter term than a usual lending format.
- Also, the credit card lender will usually reward the borrower for a shorter repay period. Many of the loans give the borrower an advantage in rates and terms by allowing the borrower to choose a shorter repay term.

HELOC Financing

More commonly known as a "home equity line of credit", the HELOC has become a popular way to borrower money for a business venture. For many years, borrowing against one's own home was known as a second mortgage and a traditional second mortgage was a set amount for a set period. The banking profession saw fit to in the last twenty-five years to allow a fluctuating line of credit against a residential property that was flexible in that the borrower could borrow up to a certain amount and repayment was similar to a credit card. (Not the rate, the payment method). There are many reasons to use this method of raising money. The rates and terms are usually much better than any commercial loan. It's easier to secure, since it is like getting a residential mortgage. (The loan is based on credit score, equity ratio and income of borrower). However, I do not recommend this method since it can easily be abused, misused and the fact that here again putting up a family treasured asset without the usual safeguards of commercial lending. Also, like the borrowing on the 401 (k) programs, there are those who are so smart and have such good business sense that using this method can actually work without a tragedy. Again, I caution anyone who does this to make sure that they know what they are doing. Think about it and then think again.

Borrow from Friends and Family

Now, you have exhausted all other options and what are left are family members and friends. I really don't think I need to tell you that it isn't always a good idea to turn to your relatives and your good friends to borrow money to start a business or for a business related loan. However, again, while I do not recommend this form of borrowing, it can work, but if it doesn't, you lose more than money. If you feel you are so skilled enough to understand your business lending situation and the ramifications of borrowing from your family, your best friends or close friends, think about it some more. Ask yourself the fundamental question, if my business proposal was not good enough for a lender, why should it be good enough for someone close to me?

Once again, this is not to say that you may succeed with your business to the level that you are successful which will allow you to easily pay back the loans. However, you should use great care in borrowing from someone close to you. I hope I don't have to tell you why.

CONCLUSION

What do all of the above methods of razing money have in common? Why do you believe I do not favor the above lending situations? Let me answer the first question by stating that the commercial lending process is such that *experts* examine a loan proposal, look at the data, look at the propensity for the deal and the borrower to succeed and come to a conclusion to loan or not to loan the money. However, even with the expert evaluations, there are always defaults, always borrowers who cannot pay back the loans.

Even with all of the safe guards of commercial lending and the due diligence by professionals, there are defaults. When you have the lack of these safeguards, the chances are greater for defaults. Who suffers when there is a default? Obviously, the lender and the borrower both suffer. If the lender and the borrower are the same, as in the 401 (k), there are those ramifications. If the lender is family and possibly close friends, there are those consequences.

Essentially, I feel very strongly that where there are little or no safeguards against a bad or weak loan, the chances are good that the loan will fail. I also believe that without the commercial lending professional setting up the loan, making provisions for pay back, collateral and all of the strict lending principles, the borrower may not have the discipline to pay the loan back in a businesslike manner. I have seen this over and over in my many years as a lending consultant and attorney.

The bottom line is make sure that you know what you are doing before you try to go outside the traditional lending process for raising money for a business or investment.

Noteworthy

- Before you go outside the traditional sources of borrowing, make sure your business plan is fool proof or you have little if any risk.
- Determine the fees necessary to borrow from 401 (k) plans before you venture there for money.
- Before you borrow from your residence, make sure you have a real solid plan for repayment that will allow a quick return and will not end up an additional burden on personal finance that you cannot meet.
- Again, before you borrow from family or friends, make sure that you completely understand your business plan and can explain to the family or friends the risk they are taking and the consequences of failure.

- If possible, if you go outside the traditional lending process, discuss your loan with a professional that can make sure you have a solid plan.

PART SIX
SBA LENDING
&
USDA LENDING

CHAPTER 33
Who is the SBA?

The *Small Business Administration* or the *SBA* is an agency of the federal government. Congress created the SBA in 1953 to encourage and provide small businesses with financial as well as managerial assistance. It exists to serve the small business community with its mission of promoting and preserving competitive free enterprise in the United States.

Historically, the SBA made loans directly to small businesses. Over time, the agency has evolved into one that usually guarantees loans made through banks or approved lenders to businesses that, for a variety of reasons, may not find credit available to them elsewhere.

The SBA's mandate is to serve small business and to encourage entrepreneurial enterprise. In order to keep the small business philosophy, the SBA established certain size guidelines.

The following represents the small businesses that the SBA has established as eligible for funding:

- Service companies and retailers with annual revenues of $3,500,000 or less.
- In manufacturing, small business means less than 500 employees.
- Wholesalers with less than 100 employees.
- $28,500,000 for most general and heavy construction industries.
- Agriculture enterprises with receipts not above $500,000 or in some cases $3,500,000 depending on the particular industry.

While most businesses can apply for an SBA guaranteed loan, there are many that are directly prohibited. Note the following excluded businesses:

- Churches
- Book publishers
- Newspapers
- Movie theaters
- Film making
- Theatrical productions
- Radio and Television businesses
- Magazines
- Businesses that promote ideas, opinions, values and thoughts
- Manufacturers of certain materials like greeting cards, books, sheet music, recordings and similar products.
- Mortgage lenders
- Lewd enterprises
- Non-profit companies

Another major requirement is that the loans be made to borrowers who are owner-occupied businesses or owner-operated real estate. The SBA does not make investment loans for real estate investors. A point to remember, the SBA defines *"owner occupation"* to mean that it requires the borrower's business to occupy at least 51 % of the total real estate being purchased using an SBA guaranteed loan. An issue, in many loans, is what constitutes the premises? Remember, before you submit an SBA loan; make sure that you account for all of the square footage, especially including basements and attics, if they can be used as business space.

Also, the SBA was established to encourage owner-occupied, small business ownership and is not for investment in real estate. If the borrower will have rental income from the property above the owner-occupied portion the SBA lender cannot use the rental income as part of the projected income to support the debt service. The borrower must prove that the owner-occupied business will support the loan without the inclusion of any rental income. Obviously, the additional income can help obtain the loan, but the SBA regulations dictate that the lender must not base the decision on the use of the investment income.

An eligibility requirement that is little known is the SBA borrower(s) cannot have too much liquidity. Could that be true? Yes, if the borrower(s) have too much liquid funds, it makes them ineligible. For example, if the loan amount is $250,000 and the borrowers have over two times the loan amount in liquidity, they are not eligible.

While it does not happen too often, I have had this situation and it is odd. So, you can have borrowers not eligible yet have a problem getting a conventional loan.

Remember, if you are unsure if your borrowers or industry, property or business is eligible; make a quick inquiry before you expend the time and effort applying. I believe that you should always prepare a loan as if it is for a conventional lender. However, if the borrower does not have the cash injection to reach an LTV of at least 75 to 80%, then the SBA loan is probably going to be the final result.

Noteworthy

- Make sure your business type qualifies for an SBA loan before you go to a lender.
- If you are unable to determine if your business qualifies, contact your nearest SBA office.
- The Borrower must occupy at least 51% of any realty to qualify for loan. Remember, the SBA is for entrepreneurial lending, not investment funding.
- All SBA loans must comply with the 51% rule and but any additional income from additional rentals helps the decision.

CHAPTER 34
General SBA Requirements

If your business can qualify under the guidelines set out previously, the loan request must demonstrate certain conditions and guidelines, most of which are similar to all commercial loans. The following is a reiteration of those principles:

- The business will be able to pay its current debts in addition to paying the new loan debt service.
- The borrower's management should have the expertise to adequately conduct the operations of the business.
- The borrower's projections are realistic and are based on the history or relevant evidence.
- There has been a reasonable amount of equity invested in the business or in the collateral pledged. There is no actual minimum collateral rule except if there is collateral then it has to be pledged.
- Credit factors have to be consistent with the successful performance of borrower's credit obligations.
- The borrower has the appropriate credit for the type of loan and the loan amount.
- The borrower is a citizen of the United States or is a Legal Permanent Resident. If the borrower is not a citizen or does not hold a green card, the borrower must prove that borrower is in the United States legally. Also, this borrower cannot own more than 50% of business and the loan must be fully collateralized and secured.
- If you are adventurous and really want to know if your loan is eligible, before you discuss the loan with a lender, you can turn directly to the regulations by reviewing SOP 50 10(5)(A). This is the basic questionnaire filled out by the lending institution whereby the SBA reviews any eligibility questions.

As you can see, the most SBA requirements, more or less, match conventional loan criteria. Obviously, there are additional eligibility requirements imposed on the lender and borrower do to the fact that the SBA is governed by government regulations. Also, you can see that the basic lending criteria are more flexible than conventional lending. However, with the SBA guaranty, the SBA lender can allow more leeway with the collateral, credit and the important LTV. Remember, the 90% LTV programs are rarely matched by any other loan program offered by conventional banks or private banks.

You should also remember, each basic SBA loan may have additional criteria. For instance, the 504 program has different loan criteria than the basic 7a program.

Obviously, the SBA fills a need for the funding of loan requests where the business and borrower have a good business plan, but may be weak in an area that would preclude a conventional bank loan. The smart borrower should always first try to acquire a loan from a conventional bank, but also consider an SBA loan.

Although SBA guaranteed loans may be more expensive and have more obligations, the fact that the SBA loan will get the borrower the funding, it makes good business sense to accept an SBA loan. I have given you a general outline of the basic guidelines, but it pays to check in detail what guidelines are necessary for your type and amount of funding request. With the ever changing landscape of commercial lending it pays to spend time looking up the present SBA eligibility requirements.

Noteworthy

- SBA loans require almost the same basic criteria as conventional loans, but offer better loan-to-value and will accept lower credit with a reasonable explanation for credit derogatories.
- SBA lenders will be more receptive to a borrower who may not have the collateral, but demonstrates the ability to carry out a well-reasoned business plan.
- The SBA will allow a first time borrower the opportunity to obtain a commercial loan.

- Be sure to check with the SBA for any particular guidelines necessary for a particular SBA loan.
- Be prepared for paying more costs and the guaranty fee.

CHAPTER 35
SBA Programs

The different programs that are offered actually define the SBA. As previously stated, the SBA does not usually loan directly to the borrowers, but make the loans available through banks or small business investment companies called *Subic's*. Subic's are federally regulated firms who receive funds from the SBA to help with start-ups or provide venture capital for expanding firms. To find these firms you can contact:

>National Association of Small
>Business Investment Companies
>1156 Fifteenth Street, NW
>Washington, DC 20005

The Small Business Act allows the SBA to administer certain defined programs. The following is a list of the most popular programs:

- 7(a) Loans
- SBA Express
- 7(m) Micro Loans
- 502 Programs
- 504 Programs
- Caplines
- Handicapped Assistance Loans
- Energy Loans
- Disaster Assistance Loans
- Pollution Control Assistance
- 8(A) Minority-owned Business Loans

Since this book is about commercial loans, I will concentrate on the primary programs that benefit the great majority of small businesses. While the SBA offers other loans, many are specially targeted loans, like those which were offered for the victims of Hurricane Katrina in 2005, I will discuss the main programs in depth. You must understand that a discussion of the SBA with all of its programs can be an entire book in and of itself.

The Basic 7a Loan Program

This is the primary loan program that serves almost every purpose. The program is used for the great majority of small business loans for straight business only financing, real estate financing, renovations, purchase, leasehold improvements, furniture, fixtures and equipment, along with working capital.

Generally, the loan amounts range from a minimum of $50,000 to a maximum of $2,000,000.

Below is the approximate financing terms:

- Real estate acquisitions/ renovation to realty up to 25 years.
- Equipment and other business assets up to 10 years.
- Leasehold improvement up to 15 years.
- Working capital up to 7 years.
- Good will up to 50% of the loan amount and to a maximum of $250,000. (Part of the change of policy with the 2009 Recovery Act.)

Interest rates are <u>variable</u> and are usually the Prime rate plus 1.5% to 2 3/4%. The prime rate used is based on the rate published in *The Wall Street Journal*. The adjustment of the rate is done monthly, which can be a benefit when the rates fall. However, remember, when the prime rate goes up, the rates also can go up.

The good news is there aren't any up front origination fees (Points), but the bad news is there is a guaranty fee for the SBA guaranty portion of the loan. Since the SBA carries a 75% or 85% guaranty, these projects to approximately 1.7% to 2.7% of the total amount borrowed. Note that periodically the guaranty fees for SBA 7a (and 504 loans) have been waived. Since the waivers of these fees are not permanent you should check to see if the fees are to be paid.

As previously stated, this program is a flexible program that can include almost all small business lending needs under the SBA lending format. Simply stated is the procedure is for the loan to be approved by an SBA lender and then the SBA issues the guaranty to that lender.

I will discuss this guaranty later but it should be noted that the most important part of the SBA program is this guaranty. This is the reason that banks can make SBA loans.

The SBA Express Program

This program is basically the same as the standard 7a except for some changes like the maximum amount is $350,000 and the lender can use own documentation. This program's major advantage is you get a quick answer but the guaranty from SBA is only 50%.

The 504 Loan Program

More complicated and at times more expensive than the basic 7(a) loan, is the 504 Loan program. This program is different from the 7 (a) program in that this program is designed primarily for real estate, equipment and machinery. Also, this program is set up for economic development and job creation. The SBA 504 program is a community lending program designed to improve the community by either:

a) Job creation or retention. One job for every $50,000 borrowed.
b) Revitalize a business district with a written revitalization program.
c) Expand minority business development, meaning business developed by 51% minority owners
d) Veteran owned and woman owned business development.
e) Other particular business development projects set out in the SBA 504 program regulations.

I have set out above some of the main criteria but the object of the program is to help, improve the economy of the area where the business is to be established. In essence, the 504 program is designed to benefit communities by job creation, diversity of business owners, stimulate stagnant business communities and assist communities hit hard by economic and budget problems.

The SBA 504 program provides long-term financing for small businesses using a two tiered system. A participating bank contributes 50 % of the funding transaction usually at the bank's conventional bank interest rate, along with the proceeds from a fixed rate debenture (Bond offering) guaranteed by the SBA. Like 7a, the borrower can receive up to 90 % loan-to-value. The debenture provides funds for the borrower at a very reasonable rate, usually below the conventional bank rate.

This program is managed through the SBA licensed Certified Development Companies (CDC) which are set up to help businesses in each state. Each company is non-profit and they work with the SBA to determine the qualification of the loan for the financing. They determine eligibility and qualification of the small business borrower and follow through with the issue of the debenture guaranteed by the SBA. The CDC does investigate and evaluate the loan requests, like the bank's due diligence. If the CDC believes the loan request is proper under all the regulations, it joins with a conventional bank to fund the transaction. I have simplified the transaction but can say that the approval by the CDC can take time since the loan must go through a longer presentation process than the SBA 7a process. However, there are many advantages to the 504 program, like the fact that loan is a fixed rate, as opposed to the 7a adjustable rate loan terms. Also, as previously stated, the overall debt payment is usually less than the conventional bank rate.

Some essentials of the program are:

- The two loans together cannot exceed 90% of the total LTV with the borrower injecting at least 10% of the loan amount.
- New business ventures will usually only qualify for an 85% LTV.
- Construction loans are permitted.
- The debentures funds are fixed rate proceeds obtained from public security markets that have a twenty-year maturity.

- Financing terms are either 10 years or 20 years.
- There is a prepayment penalty for any prepayment during the first 50% of the loan term. (Differs from 7a.)
- The 504 loan program is more restrictive than the 7a
- The 2009 Recovery Act has made changes to the SBA regulations as to good will and fees. Also, the legislation now allows for <u>refinancing or restructure of existing debt</u> under certain circumstances. You should check with the SBA at the time of application on the specific changes in the regulations and whether the changes are still in effect.
- In February of 2011, the SBA implemented a temporary refinancing program the Small Business Jobs Act of 2010 which allowed refinancing of balloon loans that mature after December 31, 2012.
- Always check the SBA website to determine what programs are available at the time needed. Also, you can always check the Federal Register to determine what up to date SBA legislation has been implemented.

Can an SBA 7a loan be combined with an SBA 504?

Since an SBA 504 can only be used for particular purposes, the borrower can use the SBA 7a program combined to finance real estate, working capital, inventory and other requests like franchise fees.

Let's start with a small business looking for a loan that includes buying a building, making renovations, and needs working capital to acquire a franchise. In our example, the borrower calculates that all told he needs $1,060,000. The borrower has less than $200,000 to make the deal. A conventional lender would want at least $250,000 cash injection and since it is a start-up, the lender would more than likely not do the deal unless the borrower had a long relationship with the lender. So, with the risk factors and the amount of cash available, the borrower could go to a combination of SBA loans.

With a combination of an SBA 7a loan and a 504 loan program, the borrower can put $159,000 into the deal and make it work. The combination loan is as follows:

Borrower $159,000 or 15%
SBA   371,000 or 35%
Bank   530,000 or 50%

As you can see, the loan can get done with a combination of programs to the benefit of the borrower.

The 7m Loan Program (Micro Loan)

Micro loan program provides short-term loans up to $35,000. This program is aimed at the purchase of inventory, supplies, equipment and fixtures. Since the amount is low, this program usually helps small businesses at the start-up phase or where the business under estimated its needs for inventory and supplies. Like the 7a program the funding is through intermediary lenders that qualify and are non-profits. Unlike the 7a loan program the loans are not guaranteed by the SBA. All the credit decisions are made at the local level. The average loan is about $10,500 with terms of six years and interest rates and cost set by the lender. Usually the terms are 4% over the prime rate.

One of the qualifications to do a Micro Loan is the lender is required to provide business training and many of the loans require that the borrower complete the business training. From the beginning of the SBA, the agency fostered the basic idea that if a borrower received benefits from the programs, it was incumbent on the agency to provide assistance with business training to help produce successful entrepreneurs.

CAPlines

SBA provides many small business programs and the CAPlines fit the profile. The CAPlines are five different short term programs that help borrowers with programs that mature in five years or under.

Seasonal lines of Credit. Must use proceeds for seasonable inventory and accounts receivable. The line can be revolving or non-revolving.

Contract Line. The line is for labor and materials on assignable contracts.

Builders Line. Like the contract line, it is for small contractors who borrow for materials and labor where project serves as collateral.

Asset Based Loans. Your standard line of credit type, which is revolving and is based on converting short-term assets into cash.

Small-Assets Based Line. Your standard line of credit up to $200,000 where the restrictions are less than standard asset based lending.

The CAPlines programs are more flexible and are a shorter term than most SBA programs but the borrowers have to be able to show the same liquidity and credit worthiness of the other programs.

Noteworthy

- Search the type of SBA loan you need and become familiar with the actual funding criteria.
- Check with a variety of SBA lenders before choosing which program to use.
- Remember, you can combine the 7a loan with the real estate based 504 loan program
- For short term loans, check with the CAPlines.
- Check out all SBA programs. There may be new programs offered that can help your business.

CHAPTER 36
SBA Fees and Interest

No one likes to pay lenders fees for borrowing money. Along with the fees charged, comes the interest structure which for most SBA loans is an adjustable rate tied to the prime rate. With the many benefits of the SBA loan programs comes a price tag, SBA fees and the interest rate can change overnight.

FEES

Reading the SBA fee schedule regulations is like looking at a Rubric's Cube. Before you can figure it out, you have to line up all the cubes. Also, the more you read the more confused you become because the fees move up and down with not only the size of the loan but the loan program. When you are use to conventional banking rates, the SBA rates and terms become even more confusing. Below are the rates and term schedules at the present time. You must remember, with the SBA, regulations can change so you must always read the current law. At the moment, the maximum guaranty fee is 2.75% of the guaranty portion of the loan.

INTEREST RATES

As previously stated, the basic SBA loan programs come with an adjustable rate based on the Wall Street Journal Prime Rate. Most of these loans adjust monthly. Yes, I said it again, <u>monthly.</u> This can have a devastating effect when you get the debt service bill after a rise in the prime rate. The sword can change into a shield when the prime rates drops, as it has done in the recent past. What I have found is the rate's up and down movement is not a detriment where you are reaching out for a loan to startup a business or your business needs a helping hand. However, you must make sure you understand the rates which are stated below and the adjustable nature of the various programs. Likewise, you must prepare your projections of debt service on the possible rates and terms.

Here are the interest and fees when asking for an SBA loan:

Maximum Guaranty Percentages:
Regular 7(a) loans of $150,000 or less...................85%
Regular 7(a) loans greater than $150,000................75%
SBA *Express* ($350,000 maximum).....................50%
SBA Patriot Express ($350,000).........................85/75%

Guaranty Fees on loans exceeding 12 months in maturity:

The Lenders pays the fee and may pass it on to the borrower after the first disbursement.

	Based on SBA Guaranteed Portion	Based on Total Loan with Standard SBA Guarantees
Loans of $150,000 or less)	2.00%	1.70%
Loans $150,001 & $700,000	3.00%	2.25%
Loans greater than $700,000	3.50%	2.625%

Loans with a guaranteed portion in excess of $1 million add an additional **.25%** guaranty fee on that portion.

The guaranty fee on a $2,000,000 SBA loan is now $53,750 with term> 1yr: $3,750 with term < 1 year.

Guaranty Fee on all loans up to 12 months in maturity is only .25%, but must be submitted with the application.

Lender Annual Service Fee: 0.55% of the outstanding balance of the SBA guaranteed portion of the loan. The fee is prorated and submitted monthly with your 1502 report

Interest Rate Limits:

Term less than 7 years   WSJ Prime & 2.25%
Term of 7 years or more   WSJ Prime & 2.75%

SBA *Express* **limits are**:

Your prime rate + 4.5% for loans over $50,000
Your prime rate + 6.5% for loans of $50,000 or less

Loans of $25,000 or less May add 2%
Loans of $25,001 or more May add 1%

The above represent the general fees and interest rates of the most popular programs. With the ever changing economic conditions, before you decide on an SBA loan, I suggest you check the SBA web site at:

Sba.gov/aboutsba/sbaprograms/elending/index.html

Noteworthy

- Make sure you are aware and account for the fees and terms for the individual SBA program you are going to use.
- Many of the fees are at the discretion of the lender and therefore you can negotiate. However, if your loan is not real strong do not expect the lender to be overly sympathetic to the lowest rate.
- Remember that the guaranty fee is based on the amount of the guaranty and not on the entire loan amount.
- Always account for the various SBA fees when you are determining your loan amount and projections.
- Always understand that SBA interest rates can adjust monthly when the prime rate adjusts.

CHAPTER 37
The SBA Loan Process

When a business borrower is seeking a commercial loan, the borrower will submit information that addresses the usual loan issues. If, however, the bank finds deficiencies in certain areas, but generally likes the loan, rather than declining the loan, the lender will seek an SBA guaranty to cover the risk. In effect, for eligible borrowers, the SBA will agree to share the risk with the bank, thereby making it possible for the bank to make loans where the bank would have otherwise passed on, without the SBA guaranty. The net result is a win-win-win situation: the bank gets to make the loan and the borrower gets the funding of the contract for acquisition. Thus, the SBA fulfills its mission.

By now you should be able to see there are distinct differences between an SBA loan and a conventional loan. As previously stated, SBA approved lenders set interest rates subject to maximum guidelines established by the SBA. For loan terms of less than 5 years, a lender may not charge a rate more than 2.25% over the Wall Street Journal's prime rate of interest; for loans over 5 years, the maximum interest is Prime plus 2.27%. Generally, the length of the loan or maturity depends on how the funds will be used. Loans for working capital are usually given for 5 to 7 years. Equipment loans may be extended for 7 to 10 years. For real estate loans, 15 to 25 year loans are standard. Loans for mixed uses will have blended maturities. These longer-term loans are one of the most significant benefits provided by the SBA. While a conventional bank would typically seek repayment over a shorter period, like 15 or 20 years, an SBA loan will usually have a longer maturity to enhance cash flow for the borrower. However, the SBA 504 will have a 20 year term.

Like most commercial loans, here are some of the important items necessary for an SBA loan request package:

- Like most business loans, the cornerstone of an application for SBA financing of a small business is a well-written business plan. While many experts feel that a well-reasoned loan request includes the same information as a business plan, I personally believe that a business plan is necessary for any substantial loan.
- Personal financial documentation for anyone with a 20% or more ownership interest in a business. SBA loans require loan guarantees by owners.
- A description of the collateral being offered to as security for the loan.
- An industry analysis, which addresses the competition.

Start-up businesses should also add month-to- month cash flow projections for the first year and annual projections for the second and third year.

Generally, the heart of any loan request is the borrower's theory or the plan by which the borrower will make a profit in order to show the lender the ability to repay the loan. The business plan is essential for any lender to make the informed decision. In many respects, the SBA lenders may rely more on the business plan, than the other factors, since the SBA loan programs are to encourage new small businesses and the SBA guaranty allows the lenders to accept a borrower with less collateral and give a loan with a higher LTV.

Noteworthy

- Like all commercial loans, the SBA loan relies on sound lending practices.
- The SBA loan process can be lengthy and structured. It relies on detailed criteria laid out by the SBA regulations.
- An SBA loan will not be given to a borrower who has bad and unexplainable credit.
- The SBA loan may rely more on the business plan since he SBA loan is there to encourage business ownership.

CHAPTER 38
The Right SBA Lender and Loan Program

If a lender determines that a borrower is eligible for an SBA guaranteed loan, the lender will determine which SBA program is most suitable. Borrowers who think they might be eligible for an SBA loan program should work with a lender that is knowledgeable about the various SBA programs and should be experienced in working with the SBA. Remember, not all SBA lenders are the same. No matter where you live, there are resources for your commercial SBA loan. You can call the SBA office in your state for a list of SBA lenders. In Appendix II, I list the offices in each state.

How do You Know Where to Go?

First of all, when you decide to look for an SBA lender, you must understand the differences between the various SBA lenders. The SBA designates the status of lenders as, Preferred Lenders, Certified Lenders and non-certified General Program Lenders.

The Preferred Lender has met the agency's individual lender requirements, plus institutional requirements for safety and soundness. For the borrower, the benefit of working with a Preferred Lender, besides the benefit of their experience, is getting a quicker decision on a loan application. Preferred Lenders have earned the right to make their own SBA loan approvals. They have shown that they can give approvals based on prior operational controls as well as a low default rate.

The Certified Lender, like the Preferred Lender can get a quicker turn-around from the agency than the non-certified lender. However, they do not occupy the same status as the Preferred Lenders. Basically, there isn't that much difference between the Preferred

Lender and Certified Lender but if you want the best service and the quickest turn around, us e a Preferred SBA Lender.

General Program Lenders are qualified to do an SBA loan, but are not Preferred or Certified. Most all banks can do an SBA loan, if they have the trained personnel, but they do have to ask the SBA for an approval. These non-certified lenders can take a month or longer to get an approval.

There are over 850 Certified SBA lenders and 450 Preferred lenders all of which can be reached by contacting the SBA. I have provided the list of SBA District offices in Appendix II. Each district can give you a list of the Certified and Preferred lenders. From the lists, you can try to find a lender who will feel comfortable with your loan.

Do You Need a Preferred Lender?

If time is important, and it usually is, the Certified Lenders and the Preferred Lenders can speed up the approval process. Generally, the process of approval can take at least two weeks, no matter who the lender. If time is extremely important, the Preferred Lender can actually get your approval in a few days. The Certified Lender can usually get you an approval in ten days, while the non-certified lender will take two to three weeks. I have found that rarely can a borrower get an approval as quickly as two to three days, but obviously, the Preferred Lender is quicker than the others. I have found that if you have a banking relationship with a bank that does SBA loans; it will help you to consider that lender. If you don't know a lender, either speak to someone who you trust and who has knowledge of the SBA or go to the SBA for assistance in providing you a list of lenders for your deal. Since time is usually part of the equation, my advice is to deal with Preferred Lenders to make sure you get your loan approved as soon as possible.

Noteworthy

- Understand that all SBA lenders are not equal and you should know the difference.
- Before submitting a loan make sure that the lender is a Preferred or Certified lender.
- Always make sure that the SBA lender has an appetite for your type of loan.

CHAPTER 39
Appling for an SBA Loan

If you recall, earlier I set out what you should do to prepare for a commercial loan. Generally, all loans require the same basic information, including the SBA loan. The SBA loan process is basically the same overall loan request procedure except for the special structured forms necessary, including the SBA Application (SBA Form 4). As previously stated, the 504 loans are done with a non-profit SBA sponsored Certified Development Company (CDC) that usually has its own application that asks the borrower for certain additional information that satisfies the loan criteria for a 504 loan.

The SBA Form 4 sets out the loan in specific terms and along with the exhibits can constitute the actual loan request. A fair reading of the form shows that this application, like most, wants all the details on the borrower, loan amount, the use of the loan proceeds and management details, such as the name and address of the legal entity being used. A new borrower should make sure the application form is complete. It is extremely important to understand the application. You will notice that the application calls for information to be attached in the form of exhibits. Pay close attention to those requests.

To make sure the SBA loan request is well received, the borrower should especially take as much time as necessary to fill out each and every form required, attach all exhibits and make sure all documents are signed, especially the tax returns. The following is a list of forms that accompany the application form. You can down load these forms from the SBA website.

- **Form 4 Schedule A-**Schedule of Collateral
- **Form 912**-Statement of Personal History
- **Form G-845**-INS Verification of Status
- **Form 1624**-Certificate of Debarment

- **Form 4506**-IRS Verification Request
- **Form 413**-Personal Financial Statement

Besides the above forms, many banks have a set of their own forms that supplement the above. When applying for an SBA loan you should first inquire what forms the lender believes are necessary and must be filed with the loan request. I have found that a lender is impressed when a borrower sends in a complete application with every detail included and all forms filled out correctly. Paying attention to detail is very important.

As a matter of my own procedures I attach my own loan request which sets out in text the details of the loan request. It is extremely important to have as much detail as possible to explain the loan.

Practical Tips

- Use the correct forms for your loan.
- Make sure all forms are filled out correctly.
- Make sure all forms are signed.
- Keep a copy of every form submitted.
- Make sure the INS (Immigration and Citizenship) form, if necessary, is filed as soon as possible and submitted to the INS for verification of immigration status.

Like all commercial loan requests, the lender will want tax returns, projections, a business plan, photos of the business or buildings and all the usual items you can attach that can reflect positively on the loan request.

Lender Approval

Should the lender preliminarily agree that the loan is one of interest; the lender will give the borrower a term sheet or LOI to gauge the borrower's interest on the specific terms of the loan offer. Many lenders do not use a term sheet but will go to the second stage if interested and issue a contingent commitment with terms and a set of requests for the borrower to satisfy. However, it more common for a preliminary stage to include a term sheet or LOI.

Should the lender send a term sheet and the borrower agrees to the terms, then the lender will begin a period of examination of the loan request in greater depth. Most lenders request the borrower sign the term sheet and send back a sum of money for third party reports, like environmental reports and appraisals. Should the lender believe the loan will work under the SBA guidelines; the lender will then issue a commitment and order the third party reports. When all of the contingencies of the commitment are satisfied, the lender will request the SBA guaranty. Later in this book, I have set out what an SBA guaranty looks like and how it is used to bring the deal to the settlement table.

As a practical matter, the only difference between most conventional loans, private bank loans and SBA loans is the SBA guaranty and the need for the SBA lender to conform to the regulations required by the SBA many of which are set out in the guaranty.

When the lender receives the guaranty, the final phase is the closing of the loan. In the next chapter I set out all the basics necessary for closing an SBA loan.

The process to obtain and close an SBA loan is arduous, detailed and can be time consuming, but to most of the borrowers that have received their funding, the SBA was about their only realistic and reasonable solution for their funding need.

Noteworthy

- Make sure your application for an SBA loan is made with the most up to date forms from both the SBA and the lender. Many lenders use own forms
- Go over your loan request in detail to determine that you have included all attachments and documents necessary and required.
- Be prepared to receive a term sheet and a request for money to pay for third party reports and fees.
- Not all lenders use term sheets. They receive the loan request and do the diligence on the loan and if they approve the loan, they issue a commitment.
- The key document in all SBA 7a loans is the guaranty, which allows the bank to close loans they would not ordinarily do.
- Since the process can take many more weeks than a conventional or private placement loan, you need to have patience and prepare all parties for the additional time.

CHAPTER 40
Anatomy of an SBA Loan Request

The best way to demonstrate the commercial lending process in general and especially the SBA loan, is to take you through a real loan from the initial borrower's loan request to the final settlement procedures and closing.

This loan scenario was an actual loan with a few changes to protect the confidentiality of the borrowers and the process they went through. Hopefully, putting the loan process together and demonstrating what occurs should bring the commercial loan process more into focus. Obviously, there will be things left out to allow a free flow of the process, but the substantial items are going to be presented.

This loan was a request by two brothers and their wives, to purchase a closed restaurant, do renovations and open for business. The borrowers are experienced restaurant operators and both brothers and wives will be working in the restaurant. The borrowers' loan request had the following facts:

Borrowers: William Smith, Barbara Smith, Robert Smith, and Brenda Smith.
Credit: Average to good 650 to 700
Experience: over 15 years owning and working in the food service industry.

Since the business plan called for buying a closed restaurant, the lenders paid particular attention to the resumes of the borrowers. Critical to the process was the fact that one of the borrowers, Robert Smith, had experience in starting up a restaurant. Robert had previously bought a failing restaurant and brought it to success. He previously had purchased a small building for less than $150,000, had renovated the interior and bought equipment for $60,000. In four years he sold the business for $395,000. Robert's brother, who had previously worked for him, joined him in the new venture and signed on the contract.

With around $325,000 cash, the borrowers decided to offer a contract.

Phase 1: The Contract for Sale

The borrowers negotiated a contract that included the following:

Liquor License	$150,000
Real Estate/ improvements	520,000
Fixtures/equipment	<u>125,000</u>
Total.......................... ......$795,000	

It is always important to know and understand that any contract for the sale of commercial property along with a business entity, be broken down into categories, like the above. Allocation of the purchase price is extremely important when applying for a commercial loan, whether it is a conventional bank loan or an SBA loan. The lender will set the loan amount based on the allocation of the real estate. For example, if the contract has both real estate and business assets, the conventional bank usually will only loan against the value of the realty. In SBA loans, the lender will loan against the entire project amount and not just against the real estate. However, the term of the loan will be broken down to reflect that part of the loan is for real estate, part for business assets and in most cases, working capital. Remember, business only asset loans are usually amortized over a 10-year period or less, while realty assets can go as high as 25 years. Note in our project above, the contract sets out the breakdown of the purchase price.

Phase 2: The Loan Amount:

As previously stated, an important consideration in the loan process is deciding what funding will be necessary and determine the loan amount. The first thing that the borrowers decided was to break down what would be the overall needs for opening the restaurant. They broke down the needs as follows:

Real estate	$520,000
Equipment/ fixtures	125,000
Liquor License	150,000
Opening inventory	15,000
Working Capital	72,000
Total Funds for start-up	$882,000

Because this project is for the opening a business, the borrowers realized that they needed working capital to pay for the opening inventory including food and beverages and to pay for the operating costs until the business produced enough profit to pay for itself.

Since the risk involved in opening a new restaurant is high, the borrowers knew the lender would want a significant cash injection. The borrowers decided to inject $282,000 in cash and to borrow $600,000. This amounts to 69% LTV to the overall projected funds necessary to do the deal. While SBA loans can be obtained with a 10% cash injection, the start-up restaurant loan is highly risky, therefore; to insure that the borrowers do obtain a loan, the situation called for a substantial cash injection beyond the 10% minimum required by SBA.

Remember, only 58% of the loan request was being used to purchase the real estate. If the borrowers used a conventional loan, rather than the SBA, they would be limited to 75% or 80% of the real estate or $416,000. Obviously, having to put up the remainder in cash would be very difficult and for most borrowers, impossible. The borrowers' only real option is the SBA 7a loan program.

Phase 3: The Loan Package:

Every loan package contains the essentials as outlined in *Chapter Three*, but a start-up business plan demands that the borrowers supply a detailed business plan with a projected cash flow based on assumptions. While cash flow projections are important in any business plan, a start-up is much more difficult since there aren't any historical business figures to present. A borrower must find comparable business figures, must rely on industry standards and other facts to support the figures projected.

In our present loan, the fact that the borrowers were experienced and operated other similar restaurants, the numbers that they projected had more validity than borrowers who may never operated or owned a similar business. However, like all projections, they have to be substantiated by solid facts.

The borrowers, using figures from their old business prepared a projected three-year profit and loss statement to support their loan request of $600,000. Along with the projections, the borrowers put in their business plan a management plan, payroll and a personnel plan, a specimen menu and a market plan with a budget. The package contained substantial demographic information about the surrounding towns; the traffic counts on the road in front of restaurant and the competition. Also, included in the package were three years tax returns and personal financial statements of all the borrowers. What stood out in importance was the tax returns for all three years showed the borrowers has successfully managed a similar restaurant for a profit.

When the lender reviewed the loan, the response was positive, but the lender requested that the borrowers agree to submit at the bank's request for an SBA Guaranty under section 7a. This was agreeable to the borrowers and they filled out the numerous forms required by the SBA and waited for an answer.

Why did the lender request an SBA guaranty? It appeared that the borrowers were very capable of carrying out the business plan. The borrowers had invested a rather large sum of money and it appeared that the loan had sufficient collateral. In addition, the credit was excellent and from all observations, the loan should have been approved. However, with the loan being a start-up restaurant loan, which can have numerous problems the bank wanted an SBA guaranty. The uncertainty of the profits and the time it takes to get to the profits was the primary risk factor. The lender knows that all restaurant loans carry a high risk factor, even with experienced borrowers.

Phase 4: The Commitment or Preliminary Approval

After three weeks of questions by the lender and answers by the borrowers, the loan was approved for the requested amount of $600,000. As stated earlier, when the lender agrees to the loan, the lender will send the borrowers a commitment. This lender did not use a term sheet or LOI.

Generally, commitments are in the form of a letter agreement. The letter was addressed to the actual borrower and the main guarantors. Note that there is an approval but the approval is preliminary and subject to the borrowers meeting contingencies.

Below is the actual commitment.

Dear Mr. Smith

We are pleased to inform you that National Bank, a Preferred Lender under the U.S. Small Business Administration ("SBA") Preferred Lender Program, has approved your request for an SBA guaranteed loan in the amount of $600.000. Your SBA loan is subject to satisfaction of all of the terms and conditions to be set forth in a SBA Loan authorization. The SBA Authorization will be issued and sent to you upon (1) your acceptance of this letter and our receipt of any required fee for the appraisals and environmental reports and (2) the issuance of a 75% guaranty of your loan by the SBA. We must receive the enclosed original copy of this later, signed by you, indicating your intent to proceed with your SBA loan request, together with the required fee, prior to July 26, 2003.

Prior to closing the SBA Loan, a satisfactory appraisal of the real estate securing this loan is required together with, when applicable, an environmental assessment of the commercial real estate.

The basic terms of our preliminary and conditional approval are as follows:
1. Borrowers:
   ABC Corporation C/O Robert Smith President
2. Amount of loan:
   $600.000
3. Terms:

21 years (Payable in 252 monthly installments with the first 3 months as interest only.)

4. Interest Rate:
Prime+ 2.5% adjustable monthly

5. Monthly Payment:
$4, 395 (EST.)
Subject to prime rate at time of SBA approval.

6. SBA Guaranty Fee: *
* $11, 250 (EST.)
* The SBA guaranty fee may be payable out of the loan proceeds.

7. Collateral:
   a) First and prior purchase money mortgage (including assignment of rents) in the amount of $600, 000 to purchase the business property commonly known as 100 Main Street, Ocean, NJ
   b) Second mortgage on Barbara and Robert Smith's single family residence commonly known as 10 Cherry Street, Ocean, New Jersey subject only to a first mortgage held by Equity Mortgage in an amount not exceeding $75, 000.
   c) Second mortgage on Brenda and William Smith's single-family residence commonly known as 10 Apple Drive, Ocean, New Jersey subject only to a first mortgage held by Countrywide in an amount not exceeding $85, 272.
   d) First Security Interest in accounts receivable; inventory; machinery and equipment; furniture and fixtures; contract rights and any other tangible and intangible assets.
   e) Pledge to Lender of 100 % of outstanding shares of stock (but not voting rights) in The Smith's Corp., the entity owning the liquor license.
   F) Assignment of certificate of deposit held by Barbara and Robert Smith in the amount of $10, 000 with acknowledgement from the issuing financial institution.

8. Use of Proceeds:
$468, 000 to acquire the business property referenced above.
$67, 000 to purchase machinery and equipment.
$15, 000 to purchase inventory.

9. Guarantor(s):

Barbara Smith, Robert Smith, Brenda Smith and William Smith

10. Life Insurance:

Term life insurance insuring the lives of Barbara Smith, Robert Smith, Brenda Smith and William Smith in the amount of $150, 000 each is required. You may wish to obtain a new policy (ies) or you may of course use an existing policy (ies) if you wish. The original Life Insurance Policy Must Be Provided at Closing. NATIONAL BANK must be named COLLATERAL ASSIGNEE under each said policy.

11. Other requirements:

1) Subject to receipt of a satisfactory appraisal of the business property to be acquired indicating a value not less than $795.000 as is, including furniture, fixtures, and equipment and liquor license. The appraisal must value the real estate of a minimum of $520, 000. Furniture, fixtures and equipment as a minimum for the three assets. The total, however, must show a combined minimum of $795,000.

2) Subject to receipt of a satisfactory appraisal of the single-family residential property commonly known as 10 Cherry Street, Ocean, NJ indicating a value not less than $170,000.

3) Subject to receipt of a satisfactory appraisal of the single-family residential property commonly known as, 10 Apple Street, Ocean, NJ indicating a value not less than $140,000.00

4) Subject to receipt of satisfactory Environmental Phase 1, as to the property described in item 17 a) above to be performed by bank appointed consultant.

5) Subject to receipt of proof of hazard coverage satisfactory in all respects to Lender.

6) Subject to receipt of proof of business interruption insurance coverage in all respects To Lender.

7) Subject to receipt of a list of all equipment and fixtures that are collateral for this loan. For items with a unit value of $500 or more, the list must include a description of each item and the serial number, if applicable.

8) Subject to receipt of proof of cash injection in the amount of $282.00 as follows; $52, 000 towards purchase of real estate, $58, 000 toward furniture, fixtures and equipment, $150, 00 towards the liquor license and $22, 000 for working capital.

9) Subject to receipt of an executed copy of Contract of Sale, which must include proof that the Seller has completed $26, 000 in improvements as per agreement?

10) Subject to receipt of lease between EPC and OC on all business premises where collateral is located with term, including options, at least as long as the term of the loan.

11) Subject to receipt of evidence that lease payments will be no greater than debt payment plus reasonable property maintenance and taxes.

12) Subject to receipt of copies of all municipal approvals authorizing the operation of this business at this location.

13) Subject to receipt of verification from Immigration and Naturalization Services (INS) for the immigration status of Robert Smith.

14) Subject to receipt of revised SBA Form 4 (Application) signed in ink. *

15) Subject to receipt of completed SBA Form 912 (Personal History) for Barbara Smith indicating dates each name was used and signed in ink. *

16) Subject to receipt of completed Environmental Questionnaire signed by principal. *

17) Subject to receipt of 2000, 2001 and 2002 personal tax returns (pg. 1) for Robert Smith signed in ink and dated. *

18) Subject to completion and submission of all required SBA forms, including but not limited to a Loan Agreement and Borrower's Certification in the form set forth in Appendix D to the SBA National 7 (a) Authorization. * Please return this item with signed pre-commitment letter.

The following items are required to complete your loan application in accordance with Lender/SBA requirements:
Appraisals- 100 Main Street, Ocean, NJ ... $2, 350
10 Cherry Street, Ocean, NJ. $275 10 Apple Drive, Ocean NJ ... $275
Environmental Testing of Phase I is required on Mortgaged Property being purchased, described in Item 7 a) $1,650.

William Johnson, Esquire of the law firm of Johnson & Johnson will be representing the Lender in connection with your SBA loan. All documents must be in form and substance satisfactory to the Lender and its attorney. The loan will close at the Lender's attorney's office. Your interests as Borrower and the interest of the Lender are or may be different and may conflict The Lender's attorney represents only the Lender. You may wish to employ an attorney of your choice to represent you in this matter. If you intend to use an attorney, please advise us as to the name, address and phone/fax numbers of your attorney on the return copy of this letter. The estimated legal fee of Lender's counsel for closing your SBA loan is $3,400. In addition, there are typical legal and closing expenses and disbursements such as postage, courier service, photocopying charges, telephone, recording and filing fees, the cost of searches, and other customary disbursements. Borrower is responsible for the Lender's legal fees and expenses in connection with this SBA loan.

GENERALLY, OBTAINING LIFE INSURANCE TAKES A CONSIDERABLE AMOUNT OF TIME. THE LENDER SUGGESTS THAT YOU APPLY FOR LIFE INSURANCE IN THE AMOUNT AS REQUIRED HEREBY, $150,000 EACH. AS SOON AS POSSIBLE. PLEASE BE AWARE. HOWEVER, THAT YOU MAY USE EXISTING LIFE INSURANCE POLICIES IF YOU DESIRE, PROVIDED THEY ARE ASSIGNABLE. THE POLICY (IES) MUST BE ASSIGNED TO THE LENDER AND THE ORIGINAL POLICY (IES) DELIVERED TO THE LENDER AT CLOSING.
THE BENEFICIARY OF THE POLICY (IES) SHOULD NOT BE THE SBA OR THE LENDER.

In addition, when providing any Insurance Policy to the Lender, please note the following is the address for the Lender and must be indicated on the policy:

> National Bank
> SBA Department
> 100 Center Plaza
> Newark, New Jersey

Furthermore, the Mortgagee clause on hazard and other such policies should indicate the mortgagee's name as: National Bank, its successors and/or assigns as there interest may appear.

If the terms of our credit approval are acceptable to you, kindly sign, date and return the enclosed Commitment Letter, together with a check in the amount of $4,550 for the required appraisal fees and environmental tests, prior to July 26, 2003. It can take several weeks to complete appraisals and environmental reports which could delay the closing of your loan.

Please be advised that the Lender will charge an overnight delivery fee on all disbursements after the closing date of the loan.

Upon the issuance of the SBA loan Authorization, the Lender's attorney will provide your attorney with a closing checklist. A copy will be faxed to your attorney. In the meantime, should either you or your attorney have any questions, please call the undersigned, Mary Jones, Vice President & Counsel or Cindy May, paralegal for the SBA Department, at (800) SBA-1010. Since the SBA loan process can sometimes be lengthy and involve considerable documentation, I suggest that you involve your attorney early in the process. We appreciate this opportunity to serve your financial needs, and we look forward to a long and mutually satisfactory relationship with you and your Company.

Mary Jones Vice President
National Bank

Now, once you have a term sheet, LOI or preliminary approval or commitment, you should pay attention to the most important parts. You should read each word, but pay particular attention to the following:

- Loan amount-review to make sure it is correct.
- Use of proceeds-make sure that the break down is correct.
- Cash injection-make sure that you have the correct amount of capital to put into the deal. Most lenders want to have the capital injection proven before they will proceed.
- The life insurance-this item can be tricky and make sure that you can get the insurance. You should apply and obtain a policy as soon as the commitment is issued.
- Appraisals-Make sure that the figures are reasonable and that the collateral will be at or near the figures the bank has put in the appraisal contingency.

- Phase I environmental-Make sure that you have followed the instructions and have cleaned up any possible problems.

It appears after a review of the terms offered by the bank that the loan amount was correct and the terms acceptable. Also, for the use of proceeds and the cash injection are the amounts requested by the borrowers.

Something that bears special attention is the request by the lender for life insurance on the borrowers. The SBA requires that all borrowers have life insurance for the loan amount. The insurance can be *"whole life,"* but most borrowers want to keep the price down so they buy *"term life."* If you have an existing life insurance policy, you can use it, rather than buying another. However, you should look into the use of the policy immediately. Many life insurance companies make it difficult and time consuming to assign the policy. If you need a new policy, start immediately, since it can take four to six weeks. I have found this item is one of the items that causes the most delays, anxiety and can be very frustrating. Another aspect of the life insurance provision is that the borrowers can use the life insurance as part of their partnership agreement or shareholder agreements, if a corporation. The life insurance can be made a provision for any buy-sell agreement between or amongst the parties. In addition, the premiums paid on the life insurance policies may also be deductible by the company. You should review this area with a tax expert and your attorney when setting up the company and planning for a buy-sell agreement.

Phase 5: The Appraisal/ Environmental Inspection

In our loan, the borrowers signed the preliminary approval or commitment and forwarded it to the lender with the required money for the appraisals and environmental testing. As a result of the testing, the report came back with evidence that the seller/owner had removed an underground tank without a permit. The lender ordered a Phase II, which caused a 30-day delay. After the subterranean site investigation the report came back negative for contamination. Since there wasn't any contamination found around the removal site, the lender moved forward.

All the collateral and properties appraised within the commitment criteria so the lender asked for the SBA to issue the Authorization.

One important issue that can be discussed at this point is once the commitment is issued; the lender should be approached on the issue of closing, even though there are contingencies left to be satisfied. Why you ask should you at this point look to prepare for closing? You will find out that the SBA closing documentation is very onerous and time consuming. If time is of the essence or a problem, the SBA closing can present an obstacle. If you feel confident in the appraisal process and the environmental inspection process, I suggest you ask the lender for a look at the closing list and begin the due diligence. You will have a distinct advantage in getting the deal to the closing table quickly. If you wait for the contingencies to be met and for the lender to secure the guaranty, you will lose precious time. Most lenders and their counsel understand the request and will usually give your attorney at least a generic list of documents needed for the closing. This is an area that a qualified commercial mortgage broker can be of service. He or she should have knowledge of the closing requirements and can assist, even before the guaranty is issued.

Phase 6: The SBA Authorization

Crucial to the SBA loan is the SBA Authorization. As previously stated, the real important part of the SBA loan is the receipt by the lender of the SBA guaranty. This gives the lender the additional comfort and insurance to accept and do the loan.

Reading the authorization, you will see the guaranty of 75% of the loan, the fee for the guaranty and the general terms.

When you read over the authorization in detail, you will see that the form basically sets out the relationship between the SBA and the lender. It also sets the same terms as the commitment and adds the necessary itemization of what is needed to close the loan.

Below is an actual SBA authorization that was used to close this loan.

U.S. Small Business Administration

AUTHORIZATION (SBA GUARANTEED LOAN)
Lender: National Bank

Jersey District Office
Two Gateway Center-15th Floor
Newark, NJ 07102-

SBA approves, under Section 7(a) of the Small Business Act as amended, Lender's application, received September 11, 2003, for SBA to guaranty 75% of a loan ("Loan") in the amount of $600,000.00 to assist:
Borrower-: (EPC) Operating Company:
1. Barbara and Robert Smith 1. Smith Corporation

All requirements in the Authorization, which refer to Borrower, also apply to any Co-Borrower.

A. THE GUARANTY FEE IS $11,250.00

Lender must pay the guaranty fee within 90 days of the approval date of this Authorization. Failure to timely pay the guaranty fee will result in cancellation of the SBA guaranty. The 9O-day deadline may not be extended. Lender must send the fee to the Small Business Administration, Denver, CO 802S9-OOOl. The remittance check must show the Loan number. No part of the guaranty fee is refundable if Lender has made any disbursement Lender may collect this fee from Borrower after initial disbursement of Loan. Borrower may use Loan proceeds to reimburse Lender for the guaranty fee.

For loans of $150,000 or less, Lender may retain 25% of the guaranty fee but must remit the remainder to SBA.

B. ONGOING SERVICING FEE:

1. Lender agrees to pay SBA an ongoing fee equal to one-quarter of one percent per year of the guaranteed portion of the outstanding balance.
2. Lender may not charge or otherwise pass through this fee to Borrower.

C. IT IS LENDER'S SOLE RESPONSIBILITY TO:

1. Close the Loan in accordance with the terms and conditions of this Authorization.

2. Obtain valid and enforceable Loan documents, including obtaining the signature or written consent of any obligor's spouse if such consent or signature if necessary to bind the marital community or create a valid lien on marital property.

3. Retain all Loan closing documents. Lender must submit these documents, along with other required documents, to SBA for review if Lender requests SBA to honor its guarantee on the Loan, or at any time SBA requests the documents for review.

D. REQUIRED FORMS:

1. Lender may use its own forms except as otherwise instructed in this Authorization. Lender must use the following SBA forms for the Loan:

SBA Form 147, Note
SBA Form 1050, Settlement Sheet, for each disbursement
SBA Form 159. Compensation Agreement, for each representative
SBA Form 722 Equal Opportunity Poster
SBA Form 193, Notice to New Borrowers
SBA Form 148L, Limited Guarantee

2. Lender may use computer-generated versions of mandatory SBA Forms, as long as these versions are exact reproductions.

3. Lender must submit completed SBA Form 159 for non-PLP loans to the SBA immediately after final disbursement

E. Contingencies- SBA issues this Authorization in reliance on representations in the Loan application, including supporting documents. The guaranty is contingent upon Lender:

1. Having and complying with a valid SBA Loan Guaranty Agreement (SBA Form 750 or SBA Form 750B for short-term loans) and any required supplemental guaranty agreements, between Lender and SBA;

2. Having paid the full guaranty fee in the time and manner required by this Authorization and the SOP;

3. Complying with the current SBA Standard Operating Procedures (SOP);

4. Making initial disbursement of the Loan no later than 6 months, and completing disbursement no later than 12 months, from the date of this Authorization, unless SBA extends the time in writing;

5. Having no evidence since the date of the Loan application, or since any preceding disbursement, of any unremedied adverse change in the financial condition, organization, management, operations, or assets of Borrower or Operating Company which would warrant withholding or not making any further disbursement, and;

6. Satisfying all of the conditions in this Authorization.

F. NOTE TERMS:

1. Maturity: This Note will mature in 21 years from date of Note.

2. Repayment of Terms: Lender must insert onto SBA Note. Form 147, to be executed by Borrower, the following terms, without modification. Lender must complete all blank terms on the Note at time of closing:

The interest rate on this Note will fluctuate. The initial interest rate is 6.5% per year. This initial rate is the prime rate on the date SBA received the loan application, plus 2.5%. The initial interest rate must remain in effect until the first change period begins.

Borrower must pay a total of 3 payments of interest only on the disbursed principal balance beginning one month from the month this Note is dated and every month thereafter; payments must be made on the first calendar day in the months they are due.

Borrower must pay principal and interest payments of $4,395.00 every month, beginning four months from the month this Note is dated; payments must be made on the first calendar day in the months they are due.

Lender will apply each installment payment first to pay interest accrued to the day Lender receives the payment, then to bring principal current, then to pay any late fees, and will apply any remaining balance to reduce principal.

The interest rate will be adjusted monthly (the" change period").

The "Prime Rate" is the prime rate in effect on the first business day of the month in which an interest rate change occurs, as published in the Wall Street Journal on the next business day.

The adjusted interest rate will be 2.5% above the Prime Rate. Lender will adjust the interest rate on the first calendar day of each change period. The change in interest rate is effective on that day whether or not Lender gives Borrower notice of the change. The initial interest rate must remain in effect until the first change period begins.

Lender must adjust the payment amount at least annually as needed to amortize principal over the remaining term of the note.

If SBA purchases the guaranteed portion of the unpaid principal balance, the interest rate: becomes fixed at the rate in effect at the time of the earliest uncured payment default. If there is no uncured payment default, the rate becomes fixed at the rate in effect at the time of purchase.

All remaining principal and accrued interest is due and payable 21 years from date of Note.

Late Charge: If a payment on this Note is more than 10 days late. Lender may charge Borrower' a late fee of up to 5% of the unpaid portion of the regularly scheduled payment.

Loan Prepayment:

Notwithstanding any provision in this Note to the contrary:

Borrower may prepay this Note. Borrower may prepay 20 percent or less of the unpaid principal balance at any time without notice. If Borrower prepays more than 20 percent and the Loan has been sold on the secondary market, borrower must:

1. ADDITIONAL CONDITIONS

1. Insurance Requirements

Prior to disbursement, Lender must require Borrower to obtain the following insurance coverage and maintain this coverage for the life of Loan:

a. Flood Insurance. If FEMA Form 81·93 reveals that any portion of the collateral is located in a special flood hazard zone, Lender must require Borrower to obtain Federal flood insurance, or other appropriate special hazard insurance, in amounts equal to the lesser of the insurable value of the property or the maximum limit of coverage available. Insurance coverage must contain a MORTGAGEE CLAUSE/LENDER'S LOSS. PAYABLE CLAUSE (Of substantial equivalent) in favor of Lender. (Borrower will be ineligible for any future SBA disaster assistance or business loan assistance if Borrower does not maintain any required flood insurance for the entire term of the Loan.)

b. Real Estate Hazard Insurance coverage on all real estate that is collateral for the Loan in the amount of the full replacement cost. If the replacement cost insurance is not available, coverage should be for maximum insurable value. Insurance coverage must contain a MORTGAGEE CLAUSE/LENDER'S LOSS PAYABLE CLAUSE (or substantial equivalent) in favor of Lender. This clause must provide that any act or neglect of the mortgagor or owner of the insured property will not invalidate the interest of Lender. The policy or endorsements must provide for at least 10 days prior written notice to Lender of policy cancellation.

c. Personal Property Hazard Insurance coverage on all equipment, fixtures or inventory that is collateral for the Loan, in the amount of full replacement costs. If full replacement cost insurance is not available, coverage should be for maximum insurable value. Insurance coverage must contain a LENDER'S LOSS PAYABLE CLAUSE in favor of Lender. This clause must provide that any act or neglect of the debtor or owner of the insured property will not invalidate the interest of Lender. The policy or endorsements must provide for at least 10 days prior written notice to Lender of policy cancellation.

d. Life Insurance, satisfactory to Lender:

(1) On the life of Barbara Smith in the amount of $300,000.00

(2) On the life Robert Smith in the amount of $300,000.00

Lender must obtain a collateral assignment of each policy with Lender as assignee. Lender must also obtain acknowledgment of the assignment by the Home Office of the insurer.

e. Liability Insurance in an amount and with an insurance company satisfactory to Lender.

f. Dram Shot/Host Liquor Liability Insurance in an amount of _____ and with an insurance company satisfactory to Lender.

g. Worker's Compensation Insurance in an amount meeting state law requirements and with an insurance company satisfactory to Lender.

Business Interruption Insurance coverage, satisfactory in all respects to Lender.

2. Environmental Requirements

a. Lender may not disburse the Loan until it has:

(1) Completed the review for potential environmental contamination required in SOP 50 10(4) ('"Environmental Investigation") on each business real property site that is:

(a) Acquired or improved with proceeds from loan, or

(b) Taken as collateral if the site represents over 50% of the value of all collateral securing the Loan; and

(2) Sufficiently minimized the risk from any adverse environmental findings discovered in the Environmental Investigation, or otherwise, as required by SOP 50 10(4). Subpart A, Chapter 5, Paragraph 7 (Environmental Conditions).

b. Lender should consult with the local SBA office where the real property collateral is located to ascertain any state or local environmental requirements.

c. Satisfactory Environmental Transaction Section Site Assessment for both commercial properties to be performed by Lender appointed environmental consultant.

3. Borrower, Guarantor and Operating Company Documents

a. Prior to closing, Lender must obtain from Borrower, Guarantor and Operating Company a current copy of each of the following as appropriate:

(1) Corporate Documents-Articles or Certificate of Incorporation (with amendments), any By-laws, Certificate of Good Standing (or equivalent). Corporate Borrowing Resolution, and if a foreign corporation, current authority to do business within this state.

(2) Limited Liability Company (LLC) Documents-Articles of Organization (with amendments), Fact Statement or Certificate of Existence, Operating Agreement, Borrowing Resolution, and evidence of registration with the appropriate authority.

(3) General Partnership Documents- Partnership Agreement, Certificate as to Partners, and Certificate of Partnership or Good Standing (or equivalent), as applicable.

(4) Limited Partnership Documents-Partnership Agreement, Certificate as to Partners, and Certificate of Partnership or Good Standing (or equivalent) as applicable, Certificate if Limited Partnership, and evidence of registration with the appropriate authority.

(5) Limited Liability Partnership (LLP) Documents-Partnership Agreement, Certificate as to Partners, Certificate of Partnership or Good Standing (or equivalent) as applicable, and evidence of registration with the appropriate authority.

(6) Trustee Certification-A Certificate from the trustee warranting that:

(a) The trust will not be revoked or substantially amended for the term of the Loan without the consent of SBA;

(b) The trustee has authority to act;

(c) The trust has the authority to borrow funds, guarantee loans, and pledge trust assets;

(d) If the trust is an Eligible Passive Company, the trustee has authority to lease the property to the Operating Company;

(e) There is nothing in the trust Agreement that would prevent Lender from realizing on any security interest in trust assets;

(f) The trust agreement has specific; language confirming the above; and

(g) The trustee has provided and will continue to provide SBA with a true and complete list of all trustors and donors.

(7) Trade Name -Documentation that Borrower has complied with state requirements for registration of Borrower's or Operating Company's trade name (or fictitious name), if one is used.

b. Prior to closing: Lender must obtain from Borrower and Operating Company:

(1) **Ownership**-Evidence that ownership and management have not changed without Lender's approval since the application was submitted.

(2) **Purchase-Sale Agreement**-Executed Purchase-Sale Agreement.

(3) **Evidence that Seller**- has completed $26,000.00 in improvements as part of the Purchase-Sale Agreement

(4) **Equipment List** -Full list of all equipment and fixtures that are collateral for this loan. For items with a unit value of $500 or more, the list must include a description of the item and the serial number.

(5) **Municipal Approvals** -Copies of all municipal approvals authorizing the operation of this business at this location.

(6) **Lease Payments**-Evidence that lease payments will be no greater than debt payment plus reasonable property maintenance and taxes.

4. Operating Information

Prior to any disbursement of Loan proceeds, Lender must obtain:

a. **Verification of Financial Information** -Lender must submit IRS Form 4506 to the Internal Revenue Service to obtain federal income tax information on Borrower or, if the Borrower is an EPC, then the Operating Company for the last 3 years (unless Borrower or Operating Company is a start-up business). If the business has been operating for more than 3 years, lender must obtain the information for all years in operation. This requirement does not include tax information for the most recent fiscal year if the fiscal year-end is within 6 months of the application date. Lender must compare the tax data received from the IRS with the financial data or tax returns submitted with the Loan application, and relied upon in approving the Loan. Borrower must resolve any significant differences to the satisfaction of Lender and SSA. Failure to resolve differences may result in cancellation of the Loan.

If the Loan involves purchase of a business or change of ownership, Lender must verify financial information provided by the seller of the business in the same manner as above.

If Lender does not receive a response from the IRS within 10 business days of submitting the SBA version of IRS Form.4506, the Lender may disburse prior to completing this verification provided that Lender bas submitted IRS Form 4506 to the IRS no later than 10 business days from the approval date of this Authorization. Lender must still perform the verification and resolve any significant differences discovered.

b. **Authority to Conduct Business** -Evidence that the Borrower and Operating Company have an Employer Identification Number and all insurance, licenses, permits and other approvals necessary to lawfully operate the business.

c. **Flood Hazard Determination**-A completed Standard Flood Hazard Determination (FEMA Form 81-93).

d. **Lease**- Current lease(s) on all business premises where collateral is located, with an adequate term, including options, appropriate to the maturity of the Loan, considering location, type of business, and type of leasehold interest.

5. Injections

Lender must obtain evidence of the injection prior to disbursement:

a. Cash Injection-At least $282,000.00 cash has been injected into the business as equity capital. This cash is for down payment on the purchase of the real estate in the amount of $52,000.00, furniture, fixtures and equipment in the amount of $58,000.00, liquor license in the amount of $150,000.00 and working capital in the amount of $22,000.00.

6. Appraisal

Prior to disbursement, and in accordance with SOP 50-10, Lender must obtain:

a. Real Estate Appraisal on the real property located at 100 Main Street USA (this appraisal must value the real estate at a minimum of $520,000.00, the FF&E at a minimum of $125,000.00 and the liquor license at a minimum of $25,000.00).,

showing a fair market value of at least $795,000.00.

b. Real Estate Appraisal on the real property located at 10 Apple Drive, USA (AS IS), showing fair market value of at least $170,000.00.

c. Real Estate Appraisal on the real property located at 10 Cherry Street, USA, showing a fair market value or at least $140,000.00.

7. Certification and Agreements

a. Lender must require Borrower and Operating Company to certify that:

(1) Receipt of Authorization-Borrower and Operating Company have received a copy of this Authorization and SBA Form 793, Notice to New SBA Borrower, from Lender; and acknowledge that:

(a) The Authorization is not a commitment by Lender-to make a loan to 'Borrower;

(b) The Authorization is between Lender and SBA and creates no third party rights or benefits to Borrower;

(c) The Note will require Borrower to give Lender prior notice of intent to prepay.

(d) If Borrower defaults on Loan, SBA may be required to pay Lender under the SBA guarantee. SBA may then seek recovery of these funds from Borrower. Under SBA regulations, 13 CFR Part 101, Borrower may not claim or assert against SBA any immunities or defenses available under local law to defeat, modify or otherwise limit Borrower's obligation to repay to SBA any funds advanced by Lender to Borrower.

(e) Payments by SBA to Lender under SBA's guaranty will not apply to the Loan account of Borrower, or diminish the indebtedness of Borrower under the Note or the obligations of any personal guarantor of the Note.

(2) Child Support- No principal who owns at least 50% of the ownership or voting interest of the company is delinquent more than 60 days under the terms of any (a) administrative order, (b) court order, or (c) repayment agreement requiring payment of child support.

(3) Current Taxes-Borrower and Operating Company are current on all federal, state, and local taxes, including but not limited to income taxes. payroll taxes, real estate taxes, and sales taxes.

(4) Environmental-For real estate located at Main Street, USA

(a) At the time Borrower submitted the Loan application, Borrower and Operating Company were in compliance with any local, state, and federal environmental laws and regulations pertaining to environmental contamination;

(b) Borrower and Operating Company have and will continue to comply with these laws and regulations;

(c) Borrower and Operating Company have no knowledge of any environmental contamination of any real or personal property pledged as collateral for the Loan which violates any such laws and regulations, (other than what was disclosed in connection with the Environmental Investigation of the property);

(d) Borrower and Operating Company assume full responsibility for all costs incurred in any clean-up of environmental contamination and agree to indemnify Lender and SBA against payment of any such costs (Lender or SBA may require Borrower and Operating Company to execute a separate indemnification agreement);

(e) Until full repayment of Loan, Borrower and Operating Company will promptly notify Lender and SBA if it knows, suspects or believes there may be any environmental contamination in or around the real property securing the Loan, or if Borrower, Operating Company or such property are subject to any investigation or enforcement action by any Governmental agency pertaining to any environmental contamination of the property.

b. Lender must require Borrower and Operating Company to certify that they will:

(1)Reimbursable Expenses-Reimburse Lender for expenses incurred in the making and administration of the Loan.

(2) Books, Records, and Reports-

(a) Keep proper books of account in a manner satisfactory to Lender;

(b) Furnish Year-end statements to Lender within 120 days of fiscal year end;

(c) Furnish additional financial statements or reports whenever Lender requests them;

(d) Allow Lender or SBA, at Borrower's or Operating Company's expense, to:

(1) Inspect and audit books, records and papers relating to Borrower's and Operating Company's financial or business condition; and

(2) Inspect and appraise any of Borrower's and Operating Company's assets; and

(3) Allow all government authorities to furnish reports of examinations, or any records pertaining to Borrower and Operating Company, upon request by Lender or SBA.

(3) Equal Opportunity-Post SBA Form 722, Equal Opportunity Poster, where it is clearly visible to employees, applicants for employment and the general public, and comply with the requirements of SBA Form 793, Notice to New SBA Borrowers.

(4) American-Made Products-To the extent practicable, purchase only American-made equipment and products with the proceeds of the Loan. .

(5) Taxes-Pay all federal, state, and local taxes, including income, payroll real estate and sales taxes of the business when they come due.

(6) Occupancy-Comply with the following provisions: (a) Borrower must lease 100% of the rentable property to Operating Company; (b) Operating, Company may sublease up to 49% of the rentable property; (c) Borrower will not use Loan proceeds to improve or renovate any of the rentable property to be sub-leased.

(7). Lender must require Borrower and Operating Company to certify that they will not, without Lender's prior written consent:

(1) **Distribution**-Make any distribution of company assets that will adversely affect the financial condition of Borrower and/or Operating Company.

(2) **Ownership Changes**-Change the ownership structure or interests in the business during the term of the Loan.

(3) **Transfer of Assets**- Sell, lease, pledge, encumber (except by purchase money liens on property acquired after the date of the Note), or otherwise dispose of any of Borrower's property or assets, except in the ordinary course of business.

Administrator

SMALL BUSINESS ADMINISTRATION

September 12, 2003
By: Thomas Jones. Vice President and Council –National Bank, Date: September 12, 2003
A Preferred Lender, as Lender and. as agent of and on behalf of the SBA for the purpose of executing this Authorization.

Phase 7: The Closing

With the lender's counsel now involved, the borrower's attorney begins the process of putting into play the final documents necessary to satisfy the SBA guaranty and the lender. Like all commercial closings or settlements, the lender will want certain information and documents produced and verified to satisfy the legal requirements necessary for the title to pass and to protect the lender's collateral lien. All lenders want is their interests protected.

After you have reviewed the documents necessary to settle (set out below), I will point out some differences between an SBA loan closing and a conventional bank closing. Now, remember, the following is a list of requests that differ from deal-to-deal and state-to-state, depending on the type of loan.

When the lender gives the go-ahead to move towards a closing, the lender instructs the lender's counsel to contact the borrower and borrower's counsel.

The following is a list of documents and items that will be the focus of the closing.

1. Corporation Documents - TO BE DETERMINED (IF APPLICABLE)
- Articles of Incorporation (with all amendments)
- By – Laws
- List of Currents directors and Officers
- Federal Employer Identification Number

2. Limited Liability Corporation/Company Documents – TO BE DETERMINE (IF APPLICABLE)
- Articles of Organization
- Operating agreement
- List of Members
- Federal Employer Identification Number

3. Certificate of assumed Name (filed with the state of New Jersey) (IF APPLICABLE)
A copy of the certificate of assumed name/fictitious name certificate for **TO BE DETERMINED.**

4. Appropriate Licenses
A copy of all appropriate business licenses required by the state of New Jersey and local agencies.

5. Li3quor License (IF APPLICABLE)
A copy of the liquor license. National Bank will require First Security Interest in the liquor license and the proceeds from any sale of the license. National Bank's Counsel will prepare the assignment documents for execution at closing.

6 Updated Business financial Statements

Updated business financial statements dated and signed within ninety days of the close date of the loan for **TO BE DETERMINED.** The financial statements may be internally prepared, but must be submitted with original signature. The most recent financial statements in our files are dated December 31, 2002

7. Draft Bank Authorization and Voided Check (from enclosed)
Please complete and sign the enclosed authorization Agreement for Automated Payments. A voided blank check for the account from which loan payments will be drafted.

8. IRS Form 4506
The Form 4506 must be completed to verify that the copies of tax returns included in the loan application conform with the actual tax returns sent to the IRS. The signed form must be sent in for **TO BE DETERMINED.**

9. Purchase/Sales Contract
An executed copy of the purchase/sales contract.

10. Payoff Statements (IF APPLICABLE)
Payoff statements for all debt being refinanced. Payoff statements should include the per diem.

11. EPC/OC Lease agreement (If applicable)
A copy of the Lease Agreement should be submitted for the property located at **TO BE DETERMINED.** This lease should be between INDIVIDUAL OR CORP., lessor, and CORP. OR LLC, lessee.

12 State Registration Certificate of Compliance
A copy of registration certificate and a copy of the most recent annual compliance test ("tightness tests") for the underground storage tanks.

13. Fuel Agreement (If Applicable)
Prior to closing the Borrower must provide an executed copy of the fuel supply agreement.

14. Equity Contribution

Prior to closing, National Bank must be able to identify the source of funds in Business accounts through a paper trail indicating money in a principal's account being withdrawn from that account deposited into the business account, or paid out to a vendor on behalf of the borrowing company. The Equity Contribution, in an amount of $282,000, can be documented by providing:

- Canceled check (i.e. copy of front and back of check, or front of check and bank statement evidencing that the check has cleared.
- Paid invoices/agreements

> NOTE: Any gift funds will require an original gift letter from the source indicating that the money is a gift and that the recipient will not have to repay said funds.

> All payments in excess of $1,000.00 must be accompanied by an itemized invoice and a signed SBA Form 159.

> **NO EXCEPTIONS WILL BE MADE REGARDING THE ABOVE EQUITY INJECTION REQUIREMENTS.**

15. Furniture, Fixtures, Machinery & Equipment Lists
- List of all furniture, fixtures, machinery & equipment that is **currently owned,** to include make, model, and serial number, if applicable, for all items valued at $500 or more.
- A list of all furniture, fixtures, machinery & equipment that **will be purchased with loan proceeds** to include make, model, and serial number, if applicable, for all items valued at $500 or more.

16. Seller/Shareholder Notes (IF APPLICABLE)
An SBA Standby Agreement (Form 155), with a copy of the ____Note, will need to be executed by the Creditor and the Borrower. National Bank's counsel will prepare the SBA Standby Agreement.

17. Evidence of Subordinated Debt (IF APPLICABLE)
A copy of the subordinated debt agreement in the amount of _____executed between SELLER and BUYER.

INSURANCE INFORMATION

18. Original Executed Collateral Assignment of Life Insurance (form(s) enclosed)
Complete all blanks with the requested information on page one

The owner of the policy signs in the space provided on page two. **This signature must be notarized.**

Have the insurance agent forward the form to the insurance company's home office for acknowledgement.

The assignment must be on National Bank's form in duplicate for each policy assigned

19. Copy of Life Insurance Certificate
In the (aggregate) amount of $500,000. On the life/lives of **PRINCIPAL #1 and PRINCIPAL #2** with an insurance company having an A.M. Best rating of not less than **"A"**. National Bank is **NOT** to be named as Beneficiary.

20. Original Life Insurance Policy
Please forward the original full policy upon receipt.

21. Commercial Hazard Insurance
Evidence of hazard insurance on the building(s) and the contents for the property(s) listed below for total replacement value(s). The policy

must name National Bank its successors and/or assigns, as their interest may apply, Servicing Department, as Mortgagee and Loss Payee under a lenders loss payable clause and must indicate that the policy cannot be terminated, canceled or materially modified by any party without a minimum of 30 days written notice to National Bank. **TO BE DETERMINED**

22. Personal Property Hazard Insurance

Evidence of hazard insurance on the business personal property(s) listed below for total replacement value(s). The policy must name **National Bank** its successors and/or assigns, as their interest may apply, Servicing Department, as Loss Payee under a lenders loss payable clause and must indicate that the policy cannot be terminated, canceled or materially modified by any party without a minimum of 30 days written notice to **National Bank**.

TO BE DETERMINED

23. Residential Hazard Insurance (IF APPLICABLE)

Evidence of hazard insurance on the business personal property(s) listed below for total replacement value(s). The policy must name **National Bank** its successors and/or assigns, as their interest may apply, Servicing Department, as Loss Payee under a lenders loss payable clause and must indicate that the policy cannot be terminated, canceled or materially modified by any party without a minimum of 30 days written notice to **National Bank**.

TO BE DETERMINED

24. Flood Insurance (IF APPLICABLE)

If the property(s) listed below is (are) in a special flood hazard area(s), as determined by a FEMA Form 81-93 (to be ordered by Lender), a Flood Insurance policy is required. The policy should insure the building and contents for no less than 100% of its appraised worth or maximum limit of coverage available:

TO BE DETERMINED (com.)

TO BE DETERMINED (res.)

25. General Liability Insurance
Evidence of liability insurance in the minimum amount of $100,000 for the Borrower(s). The policy must name **National Bank** its successors and/or assigns, as their interest may apply, as an additional insured and must indicate that the policy cannot be terminated, canceled or materially modified by any party without a minimum of 30 days written notice to **National Bank.**

26. Liquor Liability Insurance (IF APPLICABLE)
Please provide evidence of liability insurance in the minimum (To Be Determined.)

27. Tank Liability Insurance (IF APPLICABLE)
Evidence of tank liability insurance for all operating underground tanks.

28. Workers' Compensation Insurance
Evidence that workers' compensation insurance has been obtained in an amount meeting state law requirements.

29. Business Interruption Insurance
Evidence that business interruption insurance in an amount equal to six (6) months of gross revenues of the Business has been obtained.

THE FOLLOWING REQUIREMENTS WILL BE INITIATED BY NATIONAL BANK ON THE BORROWER'S BEHALF AND AT THE BORROWER'S COST:

30. INS Verification (form enclosed) (IF APPLICABLE)
National Bank will submit the signed INS verification form to the INS. Alien status must be confirmed by the INS prior to submitting to the SBA.

31. Local, State and Federal Tax Lien and Judgment Searches

These searches must be performed on Borrowers, Sellers and Guarantors.

32. State and County UCC Searches
These searches must be performed on Borrowers, Sellers and Guarantors.

33. Residential Real Estate Appraisal (IF APPLICABLE)
A residential real estate appraisal(s) for the property(s) listed below will be required prior to the close of this loan. The property must have a certified

TO BE DETERMINED,

34. Commercial Real Estate Appraisal
A commercial real estate appraisal(s) for the property(s) listed below will be required prior to the close of this loan. The property must have a certified appraised value of no less than value(s) listed. Evidence(s) of **Zoning**

Compliance for all commercial real estate collateral(s) are also required:

TO BE DETERMINED, in the amount of $

35. Environmental Assessment
A Phase 1 environmental site assessment will be required prior to Closing on all commercial properties.

36. Title Search
A title search(s) covering at least fifty (50) years must be provided for the residential/commercial property(s) listed:

TO BE DETERMINED (COM.)
TO BE DETERMINED (RES.)

37. Title Insurance

Lender's title insurance in the amount of the loan, insuring **National Bank**, its successors' and/or assigns. The title commitment should be provided for the property(s) listed below. A **survey(s)** of the commercial property(s) must be provided prior to the close of the loan if any title commitment contains a survey exception:

TO BE DETERMINED (com.)
TO BE DETERMINED (res.)

As you can see, there is a large amount of items and conditions necessary to be satisfied before the bank will close the loan. Also, please note that many of the terms and conditions have already been satisfied and met. However, it can take a number of weeks or more for all of the above to be given to lender's counsel and have approved for closing.

Some closing documents are purely legal in nature and some go to the lender's responsibility to make sure that SBA regulations have been followed. What is usually a simple due diligence in most commercial loans, become a quest in SBA closings. Why? Simply put, the lender is compelled to strict compliance do to the need to satisfy the high criteria of the SBA and the SBA loan format. What is important to the lender is the consequences should there be a default. With a default, the SBA will audit the loan to determine if the lender complied with the SBA regulations. If the lender did not comply with all the regulations, requirements, etc. the SBA can reject payment of the guaranty amount. This added element makes SBA loans different from the common commercial loan. Remember, the very essence of an SBA loan is the ability of the lender to have the added security of the SBA guaranty. It is the job of the lender's counsel to protect the lender by making sure that all of the necessary closing requirements are fulfilled.

I caution any borrower who is going through the final phase of the SBA loan. It can be frustrating and sometimes painful to seemingly repeat the same things that you already did or satisfied. Do not get angry but do what you are told to get the deal closed. It does take patience and be prepared for the procedure to be frustrating.

Lender's Counsel

Most SBA lenders will use an outside law firm not legally or professionally associated with the lender. On the smaller loans, many lenders use in-house counsel. Remember, the counsel for the lender has the responsibility to make sure that the lender is protected not only in the transaction but with the SBA. Many of the items on the previous list are specific items that are required only because the loan carries an SBA guaranty. However, the great majority of items are standard closing items that are always necessary. As a borrower you should be familiar with the items, if only, to be a help in getting the loan closed.

Practical Tips

- SBA requires life insurance on the borrowers. In our deal all four borrowers (Guarantors) have to have policies to cover the loan amount.
- Cash injection by the borrower is extremely important. Make sure the lender has verification of the funds either already injected or are ready to be injected. Need copies of bank accounts, cancelled checks or receipts.
- Closing an SBA loan can be tedious and time consuming. You should always have an attorney who is familiar with SBA closings.
- Before an actual date for the closing is set, most lenders will require all of the closing documents be approved by the lender's counsel. Do not rely on bringing important documents to the closing without the documents being approved by the lender and the lender's counsel.
- Important for a fast close is to start as soon as you feel comfortable that the appraisal contingency will be met. If you are confident that the realty or collateral offered will meet the contingency requirements, and then start working on the closing list.

As a general rule, being able to get the loan to the closing table in a two to three weeks is a credit to having the proper preparation and understanding of what is necessary for closing. Beware; rarely will an SBA closing occur in a few weeks after the guaranty is issued. Expect at least 30 days or more.

Phase 8: Closing Day

Like all loan transactions, the commercial loan settlement or closing will require the personal attendance of all borrowers. Rarely will a lender allow a closing to go ahead where a party (borrower) is not present, even if the attorney for the borrower can present a valid *Power of Attorney*, appointing someone else to sign the documents. Under certain circumstances lenders will allow a closing to go ahead where the borrower isn't present, but most of the time the documents have been signed and witnessed ahead of time. Do not rely on a last minute power of attorney. Make sure as a borrower you attend the closing.

As a practical matter, the closing should be more of a formality than a complicated procedure. If you have done the proper due diligence on the closing documents and conditions, the actual closing should be an exercise in making sure all the documents are signed and that the closing statements are correct. With the aid of counsel, all of the documents should have been read and signed with the proper financial arrangements made to satisfy the contract.

Noteworthy

- Closing an SBA loan is not like closing any other type of loan. It demands more of the borrower and the lender.
- The borrower should begin gathering closing documentation as soon as the loan is approved and should not wait until the SBA guaranty is sent if the borrower expects to close the loan in weeks not months.
- Like all closings, bring certified funds necessary for the cash injection.
- Make sure that your attorney has reviewed all-important documents.
- Double check all figures that appear on any settlement sheet or closing statement.
- Make sure that you are given a complete copy of all documents.
- Make sure you store closing documents in a safe place, preferably a bank safety-deposit box.
- Do not expect a quick closing, but if everything is done efficiently it can get done in 30 days.

CHAPTER 41
USDA Commercial Loans

I am sure if you asked most people the question, does the Department of Agriculture make commercial loans; most people would scratch their head. No, the United States Department of Agriculture does not make loans, but like the SBA, they do guarantee commercial loans for people and businesses that live in rural areas

To begin with, one of the best secrets is the USDA *Business and Industry* guaranteed loan programs. If you are a commercial loan consultant living in a rural area, the USDA B&I loan can be a great tool in your box of lending tools. Like SBA, they help make business and commercial loans much easier and like SBA, they may be your only hope of helping a client. Again, like SBA there are restrictions on the types of loans, the types of borrowers and the location of the commercial business that is requesting the loans.

Eligibility for a Loan

Probability the first item of eligibility that you should check is whether the location of the loan is in an area that USDA has determined is a *"rural area."* Since there are many definitions of the term, it is best to go to USDA web site and follow the directions using zip codes. It is quite easy to determine the eligibility of a particular area. Now, it is not just population or density, there are other factors and exceptions which means you have check the site for eligibility. The basic idea is to guarantee loans to businesses in rural areas. As a practical matter check with your USDA office to be sure. I had the unfortunate experience to have a loan rejected because it was on the wrong side of a street. As a matter of less than 100 feet, the loan didn't qualify.

Authorized Loan Purposes

Like SBA, there are particular purposes that the USDA loans are tailored. Here are some of the choices:

- Business and industrial acquisitions, construction, expansion, repair and development costs.
- Purchase of equipment, machinery and supplies.
- Startup costs and working capital.
- Pollution and environmental controls and abatement
- Purchase of startup stock for cooperative farming
- Refinancing under certain conditions.
- Special programs that USDA provides

Ineligible Business

- Owner occupied rental housing.
- Lending and investment companies.
- Pay off creditor where amount exceeds collateral.
- Finance any illegal or gambling, racetracks, gold courses.
- Finance any line of credit

The above represents some of the areas where USDA loans will not be allowed. To be sure, if you have a question, you should check with your local office.

Authorized Use of Funds

Borrower must show one of the following for the use of funds:

- Provide or keep jobs and employment
- Improve economic or environmental climate
- Promote conservation, development and use of water for agriculture
- Provide for renewable energy sources

Size of Loans

Unlike SBA whose limits are $4,000,000 the USDA has greater limits as set out below.

- No minimum
- Up to 10 million (To one borrower)
- Usual range from $200,000 to $5,000,000.
- However, there can be an exception granted under special circumstances by Administrator

Terms

Somewhat like SBA 504 loans, the lender can fix the rate but can also give a 30 year term. However, note that you will pay probably 1 basis point to lender and 2 basis points to USDA. Compared to SBA which has a guaranty fee up to 2.75 points, the difference is slight and should not be enough to discourage a borrower.

- The interest rate is the usual customary commercial rates that the lender charges its customers.
- Interest rates can be fixed or variable but cannot change more than quarterly.
- Working capital loans up to seven years.
- Equipment not more than 15 years
- Real estate not more than 30 years
- No balloons are allowed.
- Fees are the usual and customary fees and USDA charges 2 percent (Points) for guaranteed amount.
- Up to 85% LTV, usually 80% in most loans.

Credit Requirements

- Usual cash flow requirements and debt coverage, or at least 1.125 debt service ratio.
- Life Insurance on key borrowers.
- Borrowers with 20% or more interest must guarantee.
- Adequate collateral or security.

Lenders

Unlike SBA, any Federal or State Chartered Bank, Farm Credit System, Saving and Loan Associations, Insurance Company's mortgage division and Credit Unions can do these loans. Also, any lenders with commercial lending experience and proper financial strengths may be approved. As you can see, the spectrum of lending choices is much larger than SBA.

Miscellaneous Facts

In addition to the above, there are other things you should know.
- Business must be majority owned by US citizen or Permanent resident Alien.
- No government or military employees who own 20% or more are eligible.
- Project doesn't involve relocation of 50 or more employees.
- Refinance loan can include own debt but it has to be less than 50% of new loan. (Similar to SBA 504).

The Business and Industry (B&I) program is <u>lender-driven</u> --- the lender requests the guarantee, and, if approved, closes, and services the loan.

1. Standard guarantee is 75% on loans up to $5 million, 70% for loans from $5 to $10 million.
2. The guaranteed portion of the loan does not count toward the bank's legal lending limit, and the lender may sell the guaranteed portion of the loan in the secondary market to generate fee income.
3. B&I guaranteed loans help lenders satisfy Community Reinvestment Act (CRA) requirements.

4. Interest rates are negotiated between the borrower and the lender, they can be either fixed or variable, but the rate may not be adjusted more than quarterly.
5. The repayment terms for loans on real estate will not exceed 30 years, 15 years, or the useful life, for machinery and equipment, and 7 years for working capital purposes.
6. Loans with balloon payments are not permitted.
7. An existing business must have a tangible Balance Sheet equity position of 10% or more, and 20% or more for a new business.
8. The guaranteed portion of the loan does not count toward the bank's legal lending limit, and the lender may sell the guaranteed portion of the loan in the secondary market to generate fee income.
9. B&I guaranteed loans help lenders satisfy Community Reinvestment Act (CRA) requirements.
10. Interest rates are negotiated between the borrower and the lender, they can be either fixed or variable, but the rate may not be adjusted more than quarterly.
11. The repayment terms for loans on real estate will not exceed 30 years, 15 years, or the useful life, for machinery and equipment, and 7 years for working capital purposes.
12. Loans with balloon payments are not permitted.
13. An existing business must have a tangible Balance Sheet equity position of 10% or more, and 20% or more for a new business.

PART SEVEN
AFTER THE LOAN

CHAPTER 42
Not Approved?

Not every commercial loan is funded. Generally, there are a number of fundamental reasons why a commercial loan will not be approved. Most lenders are usually professional enough to not only formally notify a borrower of a turn down, but will also give details and explanations. I have found that even though most lenders tell the borrower the actual reasons; there are some turndowns that have made me scratch my head, since the reasons usually given for a tune down are:

- The borrower is not experienced enough to carry out the business plan.
- The business plan does not satisfactorily demonstrate the ability for the borrower to successfully pay back the loan.
- There is not enough collateral to offset the risk to the lender.
- The borrower hasn't the sufficient liquidity to give the lender the comfort necessary to grant the loan.
- The borrower's credit does not indicate that the borrower will be responsible enough to repay the loan.
- The loan amount and loan-to-value are too high for the collateral and income projections.
- The borrower's business or industry coupled with the economic conditions of the market will not support the loan.

Essentially, a turn down by a lender is usually based on one or more of the above items. I have found that many lenders will generally say the following words," The borrower has not demonstrated that the borrower is capable of paying back the loan." With those words, the lender usually can point to an item that leads to the turn down. You can also add to the above the words, "Too risky." Startup business loans, in certain high-risk business areas, can, by themselves, create a high risk that a lender will not choose to fund, no matter the qualifications of the borrower.

For example, during a recent real estate market slowdown, many well-qualified real estate developers were unable to obtain loans to develop residential real estate sub-divisions since the lenders felt that the market conditions presented too big a hurdle making the loans, *too risky*.

While there are many kinds and types of commercial lenders that accept all kinds of risks, the fact remains that not all loans will ever get funded. Being prepared and doing the right things can minimize that eventuality.

CHAPTER 43
After a Turndown

Again, the reality of commercial lending is that many small business owners or commercial borrowers will be turned down. The first-time borrower is especially vulnerable unless the loan request is done appropriately with an eye on meeting all of the lender's criteria. In fact, more often than not, the first time an inexperienced borrower contacts their bank for a commercial loan; they will usually run into a problem or will be turned down. Now, even after the adjustments are made or after the borrower does all he or she can do to buttress the loan, the reality is that many loans may not be funded.

As you have learned, the average conventional bank expects the borrower to present a loan with the least amount of risk. This makes it difficult for the small business borrower unless the borrower has a large amount of money on deposit with the bank.

The private lenders, in most cases, offer much higher interest and tougher terms that can result in the borrower being unable to meet the appropriate LTV and debt service ratios. Even with all of the positive aspects of the SBA loans, many borrowers find themselves left out and unable to find the money to acquire or improve their business position.

Earlier, I discussed debt funding versus equity funding. When the borrower finds that the banks and the private lenders will not loan them money, the borrower has to turn to equity funding.

One of the main problems confronted by a borrower seeking private investment is the ability to demonstrate that the business will be able to generate profits to meet the requirements of venture or private capital. However, with a startup or with a relatively new company in need of funding to bring a new concept or product to the market, an equity investor can be a savior or angel; thus, the term "*angel investor.*"

When I spoke of venture capital, I pointed out that small business owners generally do not obtain venture capital. However, many small business owners can obtain funding from private capital, if the business plan calls for the possibility of large enough profits with possible future expansion. The possibility of large profits and expansion will allow the borrower or owner to provide a return that will attract an angel investor. Since the angel is usually a person who will add their expertise, as well as funding, the borrower can try to tailor the business plan to meet the profit level that will attract an angel investor. Many funding requests get turned down by banks only to be funded by private capital with angel investors.

Like asking for a bank loan, you should follow the same path. Obviously, after being turned down by banks, you need to evaluate your entire loan request, if you haven't done this already.

The primary difference between debt finances and equity financing dictates that the business plan for equity must include a more aggressive look at profit taking. Should your plan not have the ability to earn a larger return, the angel investor network will not work. Remember, the fact that you cannot get traditional financing or even higher risk debt financing will send a signal that you have a difficult road ahead to profit. With a sober look at the business plan, the borrower, who has been turned down, must decide to give up an equity interest to attract an angel or a private investor. Many times, the amount of equity a business must give up becomes the overriding problem.

Most states have organizations that provide information on angel networks. There are many angel networks that will provide the small business owner an opportunity to present their plan to an interested forum. Usually, the networks set aside one day, a month to listen to potential funding opportunities. The hard part is getting on the agenda of these meetings. At this point, it really pays to have a professional help a borrower to find the proper network and to get that borrower an angel.

There are other options. Depending on the reason for a turn down, you may have to change the amount of cash injection, add collateral or add a partner who has more experience in your type of business. Regrettably, the addition of a new partner will lower your percentage of ownership or level of profits. However, the decision to go forward will at least provide you, as a borrower and entrepreneur, with the opportunity to get your business up and running or to save an existing business.

One last piece of advice you should follow. If you have been turned down for your loan and don't know what to do, take time to talk to a qualified commercial mortgage broker or commercial loan consultant. Even if you have been working with a broker, many times, another pair of eyes and another look by a qualified person can help you find the funding you need. Also, as a borrower having problems, maybe you should take a good look at your loan and business and find it is not a venture to pursue.

FINAL THOUGHTS

From the beginning, I have said that commercial financing can be difficult. As opposed to residential financing where there are set guidelines and comparable criteria, commercial financing is all over the board. You can send the same loan package to four lenders and all four could easily have four different opinions, different terms and two will turn you down. What makes it worse is that all four may dwell on different items in the loan package when making their decision. What does this mean? It means you should make sure you send your deal to an array of lenders. As I have pointed out, there are many levels of lenders who will look at the risk differently. However, there is one common denominator, the risks and the rewards.

Fundamental to all commercial lending is what risk a lender will tolerate and what reward is paid to the lender for giving you the loan. As a borrower it comes down to building a loan request that can demonstrate to that particular lender that the loan request is within that lender's risk tolerance. For a borrower to do this, the borrower should prepare the loan request with the fundamental understanding that for each lender, from the conventional bank to the hard moneylender, the loan package has to represent the borrower and the loan request in the best possible light.

Let me put all this into perceptive by pointing out some final thoughts you should take away.

- Check your credit and make sure it reflects your correct credit score. Also, take whatever measures necessary to correct any mistakes if you find incorrect negatives.
- Organize your financials. If a larger loan, seek a qualified accountant to help you.
- Make sure the loan amount is correct. Borrow only what you need but make sure you are borrowing enough.

- Build a complete, well-prepared loan package. Make sure your package is up to date, correct and appealing.
- Make sure you have a well-reasoned and well-supported business plan.
- If you do not hire a loan professional, research what lender will be appropriate for your loan based on the type of loan, amount of collateral and amount of the cash injected.
- Make a professional presentation of your loan to at least three lenders.
- Always cooperate with the loan officer. Make sure you do not irritate the loan officer by constantly calling. Always be patient but involved.
- If you have a loan that probably will not appeal to a conventional bank, consider the SBA, private lenders and equity based lender-investors.
- Consider sources of funding from government programs usually through economic development agencies of state and local governments.
- If you receive a commitment, and if you have any doubts or questions about the legal ramifications, engage legal counsel.
- Make sure the loan offered to you actually works with your business plan, income and profit structure. Do not get trapped into taking a hard money loan that you cannot reasonably pay back.
- Do not take on a loan, merely because it is offered. Make sure it will not be an undue burden.
- Always ask the lender to consider a non-recourse loan or ask the lender to exclude your personal loan guaranty. Only offer your private residence as collateral if it is the only opportunity to obtain a loan.
- Be very careful when taking seller (take-back) financing. Consider having an expert review the circumstances of the loan before agreeing.
- Always use legal counsel when closing a commercial loan.
- After closing a loan, make sure you understand all of your obligations to the lender, besides the payment of the debt.

- Prepare for your next loan or refinance by keeping accurate records, maintain good credit and make sure all tax filings show a favorable view of your company or business.
- If you receive a turndown, speak to the lender about what you can do to change or add to the deal to make it a better loan for that particular lender. At the very least, always find out the reasons for the turndown.
- Always remember that the process of obtaining a commercial or business loan can take a lot longer than you would expect, so start as soon as possible, be diligent and make sure you pick the best possible experts and professionals to assist you.
- Your last resort is to hire a professional loan consultant. This expert may be able to construct or change your loan request for approval. Also, most commercial loan experts have an array of lending sources that may be right for a specific loan.

Now, at this point, you should be able to prepare a well thought-out loan request, judge the strengths and weaknesses and do your best to change what is needed to present the best loan package. You should be able to understand the various levels of commercial lenders and what kinds of loans they all accept. Most importantly, you should understand the process and how it all works. However, no matter how much you think you know, I always recommend that you allow a professional to assist you. Unless you are a very gifted person and have the requisite tools, you are usually at a disadvantage without the help of people who do it for a living.

I am hoping with your knowledge from this book, you will be at least being able to protect yourself from making a poor decision in accepting a bad loan. Remember, if you keep improving your loan request and identify the right lender for your loan, you will be successful.

ACKNOWLEDGEMENTS

Over all the years involved in commercial lending as an attorney and as a loan consultant, I have had many conversations, with borrowers, lenders and counsel for both sides. Along with hands-on experience, I have voraciously read numerous books and trade articles associated with commercial lending. To sum up my sources for this book is virtually impossible. So many of my thoughts expressed in this book are from my experiences. Many are from of my fellow loan consultants and bankers. It would be impossible to thank everyone whose input eventually went into this book.

In the research for this book, I have found that the public library is by far the best source of information. In this Google-Wikipedia oriented world, I still use the library to review all of the information available on any subject. Most times I have checked more than two information sources in order to reach my opinions.

However, when it comes down to individuals, in particular, I would like to thank Steve Wortman, former Vice-President of Valley National Bank in my home state of New Jersey. Steve, now retired, has given me much insight into the banking side of commercial lending as well as all sides of the many issues we all grapple with when doing a commercial loan. Especially in the complicated world of SBA lending, his help and guidance has been invaluable professionally and personally. Also, I have met so many dedicated and professional bankers that have given me advice it would be difficult to name them all.

Also, I want to acknowledge my wife Brenda, whose help and encouragement has been there since I told her of my idea for a book. This leads me to a broader area. I believe no matter how much you think you have learned, seen and discussed, not a day goes by that there isn't something new to learn. The same applies to commercial lending. With each new day and each new deal I strive to do the best possible job for those who depend on me. At the same time I have tried to learn from each experience. This has required me to look deeper into the many areas of accounting, law, and general business nomenclatures and such. I hope I have expressed the ideas required to prove the viability of the commercial loan and the commercial lending process. This in a nutshell is why I have tried to write the best book possible to allow all to understand, maybe a little better, the difficult process of commercial lending.

Good luck!
Rich Carrell

APPENDIX 1
State Economic Development

ALABAMA

Alabama Small Business Development Consortium
Office of the State Director
2800 Milan Court, Suite 124
Birmingham, Alabama 35211
(205)943.6750

Alabama Development Office
401 Adams Avenue
Montgomery, Alabama 36104
(800)248.0033
(334)242.0400
Fax: (334)242.2414
www.ado.state.al.us
adoinfo@ado.state.al.us

ALASKA

Mr. Bill Noll
Commissioner
P.O. Box 110800
Juneau, Alaska 99811.0800
(907)465.2500
questions@commerce.state.ak.us

ARIZONA

Arizona Association for Economic Development

3003 N. Central Avenue, Suite 620
Phoenix, Arizona 85012
(602)240.2233
1.888.567.8793
Fax: (602)240.2391
myra@aaed.com
smallbiz@azcommerce.com

ARKANSAS

Arkansas Department of Economic Development
One Capital Mall
Little Rock, Arkansas 72201
(501)682.1121
1.800. ARKANSAS
Fax: (501)682.7394
INFO@1800ARKANSAS.COM

CALIFORNIA

California Business Investment Services (CalBIS)
CalBIS
801 K Street, Suite 2100
Sacramento, California 95814
(916)322.0000
Fax: (916)322.0614
CalBIS@labor.ca.gov

COLORADO

Office of Economic Development and International Trade
1625 Broadway, Suite 1700
Denver, Colorado 80202
(303)892.3840
Fax: (303)892.3848
www.state.co.us

CONNECTICUT

Department of Economic and Community Development
505 Hudson Street
Hartford, Connecticut 06106
(860)270.8000
DECD@po.state.ct.us

DELAWARE

Delaware Economic Development Office
99 Kings Highway
Dover, Delaware 19901
(302)739.4271
Fax: (302)577.8499
Delaware Economic Development Office
802 French Street
Wilmington, Delaware 19801
(302)577.8477
Fax: (302)577.8499
Judy.cherry@state.de.us

DISTRICT OF COLUMBIA
Washington, DC

DC Marketing Center
1495 F Street, NW
Washington, DC 20004
(202)661.8670
Fax: (202)661.8671
www.dcmarketingcenter.com

FLORIDA

Florida Economic Development Council, Inc.
P.O. Box 3186
Tallahassee, Florida 32315.3186

(850)201.FEDC
Fax: (850)201.3330

Florida Economic Development Council, Inc.
The Atrium Building
325 John Knox Road, Suite 201
Tallahassee, Florida 32303
info@fedc.net

GEORGIA

The Georgia Department of Economic Development
75 Fifth Street, N.W., Suite 1200
Atlanta, Georgia 30308
(404)962.4000
www.georgia.org

HAWAII

Department of Business, Economic Development and Tourism
P.O. Box 2359
Honolulu, Hawaii 96804
No. 1 Capitol District Building
250 S. Hotel Street
Honolulu, Hawaii 96813
(808)586.2423
Fax: (808)587.2790
library@dbedt.hawaii.gov

IDAHO

Boise Valley Economic Partnership
BVEP SERVICES
250 S. 5th Street, Suite 800
P.O. Box 2368
Boise, Idaho 83701

(208)472.5230
sboyce@bvep.org

ILLINOIS

Department of Commerce and Economical Development
Community Development
620 E. Adams
Springfield, Illinois 62701
(217)782.6174
TDD: (800)785.6055
gwilliams@ildceo.net

INDIANA

Indiana Economic Development Corporation
One North Capitol, Suite 700
Indianapolis, Indiana 46204
(312)332.8800
Fax: (317)232.4146
cpfaff@iedc.in.gv

IOWA

Iowa Department of Economic Development
200 East Grand Avenue
Des Moines, Iowa 50309
+1.515.242.4700
Fax: (+1.515)242.4809

KANSAS

Kansas Department of Commerce
1000 S.W. Jackson Street, Suite 100
Topeka, Kansas 66612.1354
(785)296.3481
Fax: (785)296.5055

KENTUCKY

Capital Access Corporation-Kentucky
120 Webster Street, Suite 330-332
Louisville, Kentucky 40206
(502)584.2175
1.888.858.8019
ChuckWillis@ky.gov

LOUISIANA

Louisiana Economic Development
P.O. Box 94185
Baton Rouge, Louisiana 70804-9185
(225)342.3000
800.450.8115
www.lded.state.la.us

MAINE

Department of Economic and Community Development
(207)624.9800
www.econdevmaine.com

State Administrative Offices at University of Southern Maine
68 High Street, 2nd Floor
Portland, Maine 04104
(207)780.4420
Fax: (207)780.4810
www.mainesbdc@usm.maine.edu

MARYLAND

Maryland Department of Business and Economic Development
217 East Redwood Street
Baltimore, Maryland 21201

(410)767.6300
1.888. ChooseMD
www.choosemaryland.org

MASSACHUSETTS

Massachusetts Alliance for Economic Development (MAED)
892 Worcester Street
Wellesley, Massachusetts 02482
(781)489.6262
Fax: (781)489.6263
www.mass.gov

MICHIGAN

Michigan Economic Development Corporation
300 North Washington Square
Lansing, Michigan 48913
www.michigan.org

MINNESOTA

Economic Development Association of Minnesota
1000 Westgate drive, Suite 252
St. Paul, Minnesota 55114
(651)290.6296
Fax: (651)290.2266
erice@ewald.com

MISSISSIPPI

Mississippi Development Authority
P.O. Box 849
Jackson, Mississippi 39205
(601)359.3449
Fax: (601)359.2832
www.mississippi.org

MISSOURI

Missouri Department of Economic Development
301 West High Street
P.O. Box 1157
Jefferson City, Missouri 65102
(573)751.4962
Fax: 573)526.7700
www.ecodev.ded.mo.gov

MONTANA

Montana Community Development Division
301 South Park Avenue
P.O. Box 200523
Helena, Montana 59620-0523
(406)841.2771
Fax: (406)841.2771
www.comdec@mt.gov

NEBRASKA

Nebraska Department of Economic Development
P.O. Box 94666
301 Centennial Mall South
Lincoln, Nebraska 68509-4666
(800)426.6505
Fax: (402)471.3778
www.neded.org

NEVADA

Nevada Commission on Economic Development
A Nevada Agency
108 East Proctor
Carson City, Nevada 89701
(775)687.4325

(775)687.4450

Nevada Commission on Economic Development
555 East Washington
Las Vegas, Nevada 89101
(702)486.2700
(702)486.2701
(800)336.1600
www.expand2nevada.com

NEW HAMPSHIRE

NH Department of Resources and Economic Development
P.O. Box 1856
172 Pembroke Road
Concord, New Hampshire 3302-1856
(603)271.2411
(603)271.2341
Fax: (603)271.2629
www.info@nheconomy.com

NEW JERSEY

New Jersey Economic Development Authority
P.O. Box 990
Trenton, New Jersey 08625-0990
(609)292.1800
(609)777.0885
www.state.nj.us

NEW MEXICO

New Mexico Economic Development Department
1100 St. Francis Drive, Suite 1060
Santé Fe, New Mexico 87505
(505)827.0300
(800)374.3061

Fax: (505)827.0328
www.edd.info@state.nm.us

NEW YORK

New York State Economic Development Council19 Dove Street, Suite 101
Albany, New York 12210
(518)426.4058
(518)426.4059
www.mcmahon@nysedc.org

NORTH CAROLINA

North Carolina Economic Developers' Association
1201 Edwards Mill Road, Suite 102
Raleigh, North Carolina 27607
(888)24NCEDA
Fax: (919)882.1902
www.nceda.org

NORTH DAKOTA

Economic Development Association of North Dakota
P.O. Box 2639
Bismarck, North Dakota 58502
(701)222.0929
www.ednd@ednd.org

OHIO

Ohio Department of Development
77 South High Street
Columbus, Ohio 43215-6130
Ohio Department of Development
P.O. Box 1001
Columbus, Ohio 43216-1001

(800)848.1300
(614)466.4551
www.odod.state.us

OKLAHOMA

Oklahoma Professional Economic Development Council
330 N.E. 10th Street
Oklahoma City, Oklahoma 73104-3220
(405)235.3669
Fax: (405)235.3670
www.okstatechamber.com

OREGON

Oregon Economic and Community Development Department
775 Summer Street, NE, Suite 200
Salem, Oregon 97301-1280
(503)98630123
(800)735.2900
www.econ.state.or.us

PENNSYLVANIA

Pennsylvania Department of Economic Development Association
908 North Second Street
Harrisburg, Pennsylvania 17102
(717)441.6047
Fax: (717)236.2046
www.info@peda.org

RHODE ISLAND

Rhode Island Economic Development Corporation
One West Exchange Street
Providence, Rhode Island 02903

(401)222.2601
Fax: (401)222.2102
www.info@reidc.com

SOUTH CAROLINA

South Carolina Economic Developers' Association
P.O. Box 1763
Columbia, South Carolina 29202
(803)929.0305
Fax: (803)252.0589
www.sceda.org

SOUTH DAKOTA

Governor's Office of Economic Development
711 East Wells Avenue
Pierre, SD 57501-3369
(605)773-3301
(800)872-6190
goedinfo@state.sd.us

TENNESSEE

Tennessee Department of Economic and Community Development
312 Eighth Avenue North
Nashville, Tennessee 37243-0405
(615)741.1888
Fax: (615)741.7306
www.state.tn.us

TEXAS

Office of the Governor
P.O. Box 12428
Austin, Texas 78711
(512)463.2000

Fax: (512)463.1849
www.govenor.state.tx.us

UTAH

Economic Development Corporation of Utah
201 South Main Street, Suite 2010
Salt Lake City, Utah 84111
(801)328.8824
Fax: (801)531.1460
(800)574.UTAH
www.edutah.org

VERMONT

Vermont Department of Economic Development
National Life Building, Drawer 20
Montpelier, Vermont 05620-0501
(802)828.3080
(802)828.3258
www.infor@thinkvermont.com

VIRGINIA

Virginia Economic Development Partnership
901 East Byrd Street
P.O. Box 798
Richmond, Virginia 23218-0798
(804)545.5700
(804)545.5600
www.yesvirginia.org

WASHINGTON

Washington Economic Development Association
10 North Post Street, Suite 650
Spokane, Washington 99201

(509)777.0525
Fax: (509)777.1502
www.mdulin@wedaonline.org

APPENDIX II
SBA Offices

ALABAMA

Birmingham District Office
801 Tom Martin Drive, Suite #201
Birmingham, AL 35211
Phone: (205) 290-7101
Fax: (205) 290-7404

ALASKA

Anchorage District Office
510 L Street, Suite 310
Anchorage, AK 99501-1952
(907) 271-4022

ARIZONA

Phoenix District Office
2828 North Central Ave,
Suite 800
Phoenix, Arizona 85004-1093
Telephone: 602.745.7200
Facsimile: 602.745.7210

ARKANSAS

Little Rock District Office
2120 Riverfront Drive, Suite 250
Little Rock, AR 72202-1796
Telephone: (501) 324-7379

Facsimile: (501) 324-7394

CALIFORNIA

Fresno District Office
2719 North Air Fresno Drive, Suite 200
Fresno, CA 93727
Phone: (559) 487-5791
Fax: (559) 487-5636
Toll free call (800) 359-1833 then press 6

Los Angeles District Office
330 North Brand, Suite 1200
Glendale, CA 91203
(818) 552-3215

Sacramento District Office
650 Capitol Mall, suite 7-500
Sacramento, CA 95814
(916) 930-3700 Phone
(916) 930-3737 Fax

San Diego District Office
550West C Street, Suite 550
San Diego, CA 92101
(619) 557-7250
FAX: (619) 557-5894
TTY: (619) 557-6998

San Francisco District Office
455 Market Street, 6th Floor
San Francisco, CA
94105-2420
(415) 744-6820

Santa Ana District Office
200 W Santa Ana Blvd.

Suite 700
Santa Ana, CA 92701
(714) 550-7420
Fax (714) 550-0191

COLORADO

Denver District Office
721 19th Street, Suite 426
Denver, CO 80202
Phone: (303) 844-2607

CONNECTICUT

Hartford District Office
330 Main Street, Second Floor
Hartford, CT 06106
(860) 240-4700

DELAWARE

Wilmington District Office
1007 N. Orange Street, Suite 1120
Wilmington, DE 19801-1232
(302) 573-6294

FLORIDA

Jacksonville District Office
7825 Baymeadows Way, Suite 100B
Jacksonville, FL 32256 - 7504
(904) 443-1900

Miami District Office
100 S. Biscayne Blvd - 7th Floor
Miami, FL 33131
(305)536-5521

FAX (305)536-5058

GEORGIA

Georgia District Office
233 Peachtree Street, NE, Suite 1900
Atlanta, GA 30303
(404) 331-0100

HAWAII

Honolulu District Office
300 Ala Moana Blvd
Room 2-235
Box 50207
Honolulu, Hawaii 96850
Phone (808) 541-2990
Fax (808) 541-2976

IDAHO

Boise District Office
380 East Park center Blvd., Suite 330
Boise, Idaho 83706
Phone: (208) 334-1696
Fax: (208) 334-9353

ILLINOIS

Chicago District Office
500 W. Madison Street, Suite 1250
Chicago, Illinois 60661-2511
(312) 353-4528 Fax (312) 886-5688

ILLINOIS

Chicago District Office

3330 Ginger Creek Road, Suite B
Springfield, IL 62711
(217) 793-5020 Fax (217) 793-5025

INDIANA

Indianapolis District Office
8500 Keystone Crossing, Suite 400
Indianapolis, IN 46240
(317) 226-7272

IOWA

Cedar Rapids, IA District Office
Des Moines Office
210 Walnut St, Rm 749
Des Moines, IA 50309-4106
(515) 284-4422

IOWA

Cedar Rapids Office
2750 1st Avenue NE, Suite 350
Cedar Rapids IA 52402-4831
(319) 362-6405

Des Moines, IA District Office
Des Moines Office
210 Walnut St, Rm 749
Des Moines, IA 50309-4106
(515) 284-4422

Cedar Rapids Office
2750 1st Avenue NE, Suite 350
Cedar Rapids IA 52402-4831
(319) 362-6405

KANSAS

Wichita District Office
271 W 3rd ST, N STE 2500
Wichita, KS 67202
(316)269-6616

KENTUCKY

Louisville District Office
600 Dr. Martin Luther King Jr. Place, Rm 188
Louisville, KY 40202-2254
(502) 582-5971

LOUISIANA

New Orleans District Office
365 Canal St., Suite 2820
New Orleans, LA 70130
Phone: (504) 589-6685

MAINE

Augusta District Office
Edmund S. Muskie Federal Building, Room 512
68 Sewall Street
Augusta, ME 04330
(207) 622-8274

MARYLAND

Baltimore District Office
City Crescent Building, 6th Floor
10 South Howard Street
Baltimore, Maryland 21201
(410) 962-4392

MASSACHUSETTS

Boston District Office
10 Causeway Street, Room 265
Boston, MA 02222
(617) 565-5590

MICHIGAN

Detroit District Office
477 Michigan Avenue
Suite 515, McNamara Building
Detroit, Michigan 48226
(313) 226-6075

MINNESOTA

Minneapolis District Office
100 North Sixth Street
Suite 210-C Butler Square
Minneapolis, Minnesota 55403
Ph: (612) 370-2324
Fax: (612) 370-2303

MISSISSIPPI

Jackson District Office
AmSouth Bank Plaza
210 E. Capitol Street, Suite 900
Jackson, Mississippi 39201
PH: (601) 965-4378
FAX: (601) 965-5629
or (601) 965-4294

MISSISSIPPI
Gulfport Branch Office
Gulf Coast Business Technology Center

1636 Popps Ferry Road, Suite 203
Biloxi, Mississippi 39532
PH: (228) 863-4449
FAX: (228) 864-0179
(Temporary Location)

MISSOURI

Kansas City, MO District Office
1000 Walnut, Suite 530
Kansas City, Missouri 64105
(816) 426-4900

St. Louis, MO District Office
200 North Broadway, Suite 1500
St. Louis, MO 63102
Phone: (314)539-6600
Fax: (314)539-3785

MONTANA

Helena District Office
10 West 15th Street Suite 1100
Helena, MT 59626
Phone: (406) 441-1081
Fax: (406) 441-1090

NEBRASKA
Omaha District Office
11145 Mill Valley Rd.
Omaha, NE 68154
(402)221-4691

NEVADA

Las Vegas District Office
400 South 4th Street

Suite 250
Las Vegas, NV 89101
Phone: (702) 388-6611
Fax: (702) 388-6469

NEW HAMPSHIRE

Concord District Office
JC Cleveland Federal Building
55 Pleasant Street, Suite 3101
Concord, NH 03301
Phone: (603) 225-1400
Fax: (603) 225-1409

NEW JERSEY

New Jersey District Office
Two Gateway Center, 15th Floor
Newark, New Jersey 07102
(973)645-2434

NEW MEXICO

Albuquerque District Office
625 Silver SW Suite 320
Albuquerque, NM 87102
Voice (505) 248-8225
Fax (505) 248-8246

NEW YORK

Buffalo District Office
Niagara Center
130 S. Elmwood Avenue, Suite 540
Buffalo, New York 14202
(716) 551-4301 Phone
(716) 551-4418 Fax

New York District Office
26 Federal Plaza, Suite 3100
New York, NY 10278
(212) 264-4354 Phone
(212) 264-4963 Fax

Syracuse District Office
401 S. Salina Street 5th Floor
Syracuse, New York 13202
(315) 471-9393 Phone
(315) 471-9288 Fax

NORTH CAROLINA

Charlotte District Office
6302 Fairview Road, Suite 300
Charlotte, NC 28210-2227
(704) 344-6563 Phone
(704) 344-6769 Fax

NORTH DAKOTA

Fargo District Office
657 2nd Avenue North, Room 218
P.O. Box 3086
Fargo, North Dakota 58108-3086
Ph: (701)239-5131
Fax: (701)239-5645

OHIO

Cleveland, OH District Office
1350 Euclid Avenue, Suite 211
Cleveland, OH 44115
Phone: (216) 522-4180
Fax: (216) 522-2038
TDD: (216) 522-8350

Columbus, OH District Office
NEW! - 401 N. Front St. Suite 200
Columbus, Ohio 43215
(614) 469-6860

OKLAHOMA

Oklahoma City District Office
Federal Building
301 NW 6th St
Oklahoma City, OK 73102
Phone: (405) 609-8000

OREGON

Portland District Office
601 SW Second Avenue, Suite 950
Portland, Oregon 97204-3192
Phone: (503) 326-2682
Fax: (503) 326-2808

PENNSYLVANIA

Philadelphia District Office
Robert N.C. Nix Federal Building
900 Market Street, 5th Floor
Philadelphia, PA 19107
(215) 580-2SBA
(215) 580-2722

Pittsburgh District Office
411 Seventh Avenue
Suite 1450
Pittsburgh, PA 15219
(412) 395-6560

RHODE ISLAND

Providence District Office
380 Westminster Street, Room 511
Providence, RI 02903
(401) 528-4561

SOUTH CAROLINA

Columbia District Office
1835 Assembly Street, Room 1425
Columbia, South Carolina 29201
(803) 765-5377
(803) 765-5962 (Fax)

SOUTH DAKOTA

Sioux Falls District Office
2329 N. Career Ave., Suite 105
Sioux Falls, SD 57107
(605) 330-4243
FAX: (605) 330-4215
TTY/TDD: (605) 331-3527

TENNESSEE

Nashville District Office
50 Vantage Way, Suite 201
Nashville, TN 37228
615/736-5881 Phone | 615/736-7232 Fax
615/736-2499 TTY/TDD Number

TEXAS

El Paso District Office
10737 Gateway West
El Paso, TX 79935
(915)633-7001
(915)633-7005 Fax

Dallas/Fort Worth District Office
4300 Amon Carter Blvd. Suite 114
Fort Worth, Texas 76155
(817) 684-5500 Phone
(817) 684-5516 Fax

Harlingen District Office
222 East Van Buren Street, Suite 500
Harlingen, TX 78550
Hrs 8:00 am - 4:30 pm
956.427.8533

Corpus Christi Branch Office
3649 Leopard Street, Suite 411
Corpus Christi, TX 78408
Hrs 8:00 am - 4:30 pm
361.879.0017

Houston District Office
8701 S. Gessner Drive, Suite 1200
Houston, Texas 77074
713.773.6500
Fax 713.773.6550

Lubbock District Office
1205 Texas Avenue
Room 408
Lubbock, TX. 79401-2693
Phone: (806) 472-7462
Fax: (806) 472-7487

San Antonio District Office
17319 San Pedro, Suite 200
San Antonio, Texas 78232-1411
Phone: 210-403-5900
Fax: 210-403-5936
TDD: 210-403-5933

UTAH

Salt Lake City District Office
125 South State Street, Room 2227
Salt Lake City, UT 84138
(801) 524-3209

VIRGINIA

Richmond District Office
400 North 8th Street
Federal Bldg., Suite 1150
P.O. Box 10126
Richmond, VA 23240-0126
(804) 771-2400 Fax 771-2764

VERMONT

Montpelier District Office
87 State Street, Room 205
Montpelier, VT 05601
(802) 828-4422

WASHINGTON

Seattle District Office
2401 Fourth Avenue, Suite 450
Seattle, WA 98121
206-553-7310

WASHINGTON

Spokane Branch Office
801 W. Riverside Avenue, Suite 200
Spokane, WA 99201
509-353-2800

WASHINGTON, D.C.

Washington District Office
740 15th Street NW, Suite 300
Washington, D.C. 20005-3544
Phone: (202) 272-0345

WEST VIRGINA

Clarksburg District Office
320 West Pike Street, Suite 330
Clarksburg, WV 26301
(304) 623-5631
Fax: (304) 623-0023

WISCONSIN

Madison/Milwaukee District Office
740 Regent Street, Suite 100
Madison, WI 53715
(608) 441-5263 Fax (608) 441-5541
310 West Wisconsin Ave. Room 400
Milwaukee, WI 53203
(414) 297-3941 Fax (414) 297-1377

WYOMING

Casper District Office
100 East B Street
Federal Building, Room 4001
P.O. Box 44001
Casper, WY 82602-5013
(307)261-6500
(800) 776-9144, Ext. 1

PUERTO RICO

Puerto Rico District Office
252 Ponce de Leon Ave.
Citibank Tower, Suite 200
San Juan, PR 00918
(787)766-5572 or (800)669-8049
Fax(787)766-5309

Puerto Rico District Office
St. Croix Post of Duty
Sunny Isle Professional Building
Suites 5 & 6
St. Croix, USVI 00830
(340) 778-5380 or (800)669-8049
(340) 778-1102

APPENDIX III
Glossary of Terms

Abstract of Judgment law: The summary of a court judgment that creates a lien against a property when filed with the county recorder.

Accelerated cost recovery system: A tax calculation that provides greater depreciation in the early years of ownership of real estate or personal property.

Acceleration clause: A provision that gives a lender the right to collect the balance of a loan if a borrower misses a payment.

Accelerated depreciation: A bookkeeping method that depreciates property faster in the early years of ownership.

Additional principal payment: Extra money included in the monthly payment to help reduce the principal and shorten the term of the loan.

Add-on interest: The interest a borrower pays on the principal for the duration of the loan.

Adjustable-rate mortgage (ARM): A loan with an interest rate that is periodically adjusted to reflect changes in a specified financial index.

Adjusted cost basis: The cost of any improvements the seller makes to the property. Deducting the cost from the original sales price provides the profit or loss of a home when sold.

Adjustment period: The amount of time between interest rate adjustments in an adjustable-rate mortgage.

Alienation clause: A provision that requires the borrower to pay the balance of the loan in a lump sum after the property is sold or transferred.

Alternative mortgage: Any home loan that does not conform to a standard fixed-rate mortgage.

American Society of Home Inspectors: The American Society of Home Inspectors is a professional association of independent home inspectors. Phone: (800) 743-2744

Americans with disabilities Act: A law passed in 1990 that outlaws discrimination against a person with a disability in housing, public accommodations, employment, government services, transportation and telecommunications.

Amortization: The process of paying the principal and interest on a loan through regularly scheduled payments.

Amortization tables: Mathematical tables that lenders use to calculate a borrower's monthly payment.

Annual mortgagor statement: A yearly statement to borrowers that details the remaining principal and amounts paid for taxes and interest.

Annual Percentage: Rate (APR): The cost of the loan expressed as a yearly rate on the balance of the loan.

Annuity: The payment of a fixed sum to an investor at regular intervals.

Anticipatory breach: A communication that informs a party that the obligations of the original contract will not be fulfilled.

Application: A document that details a potential borrower's income, debt and other obligations to determine credit worthiness.

Application fee: The fee that a lender charges to process a loan application.

Appraisal: An opinion of the value of a property at a given point in time.

Appraisal fee: The fee that an appraiser charges to estimate the market value of the property.

Appraised value: An opinion of the current market value of a property.

Assets: Items of value, which include cash, real estate, securities and investments.

Assumable mortgage: A mortgage that can be transferred to another borrower.

Assumption clause: A provision that allows a buyer to take responsibility for the mortgage from a seller.

Assumption fee: A fee the lender charges to process new records for a buyer who assumes and existing loan.

Aviation easement: An easement over private property near an airport that limits the height of structures and trees.

Back title letter: A letter that a title insurance company gives to an attorney who then examines the title for insurance purposes.

Balance sheet: A statement that shows the assets, liabilities and net worth of an individual.

Balloon loan: A mortgage in which monthly installments are not large enough to repay the loan by he end of the term. As a result, the final payment due is the lump sum of the remaining principal.

Balloon payment: The final lump sum payment due at the end of a balloon mortgage.

Basis Point: A basis point is one one-hundredth of one percentage point. For example, the difference between a loan at 8.25 percent and a mortgage at 8.37 percent is 12 basis points.

Blanket mortgage: A mortgage that covers more than one property owned by the same borrower.

Break-even point: The point in which the owner's rental income matches expenses and debt.

Bridge loan: A short-term loan for borrowers who need more time to find permanent financing.

Buy-down mortgage: A loan in which the lender receives a premium as an inducement to reduce the interest rate during the early years of the mortgage.

Call option: A clause in a loan agreement that allows a lender to ask for the balance at any time.

Capital: Money used to create income, such as funds invested in rental property.

Capitalization: A mathematical formula that investors use to compute the value of a property based on net income.

Capitalization rate: rate of return estimated the percentage from the net income of a piece of property.

Cash flow: The amount of cash a rental property investor receives after deducting operating expenses and loan payment from gross income.

Cash-out refinance: The refinancing of a mortgage in which the money received from the new loan is greater than the amount due on the old loan. The borrower can use the extra funds in any manner.

Certificate of deposit (CD): A document, which shows that the bearer has specified amount of money on deposit with a bank, stock-brokerage firm or other financial institution.

Certificate of deposit index: An index based on the interest rates on six-month CDs. It is used to determine the interest rate for some adjustable-rate mortgages.

Chattel mortgage: A lien on personal property used collateral for a loan.

Closing costs: Expenses incidental to the sale of real estate, including loan, title and appraisal fees.

Closing statement: A document, which details the final financial settlement between a buyer and seller and the costs paid by each party.

Co-maker: A person who signs a promissory note with the borrower and assumes responsibility for the loan.

Commercial bank: A financial institution that provides a broad range of services, from checking and savings accounts to business loans and credit cards.

Commercial property: An area that is zoned for business.

Commitment: A promise by a lender to make a loan with specific terms for a specified period.

Commitment fee: The fee a lender charges for promising to make a loan.

Community Reinvestment Act: A federal law that encourages financial institutions to loan money in the neighborhoods where minority depositors live.

Compound interest: The interest paid on the principal balance in a mortgage and on the accrued and unpaid interest of the loan.

Conditional commitment: A promise by a lender to make a loan if the borrower meets certain conditions.

Construction loan: Short-term loan a lender makes for the construction of homes and buildings. The lender disburses the funds in stages.

Construction to permanent loan: The conversion of a construction loan to a longer-term traditional mortgage after construction has been completed.

Consumer Credit Counseling Service (CCCS): A nationwide, nonprofit organization that helps consumers get out of debt and improve their credit profile. National headquarters: 8701 Georgia Avenue, Suite 507. Silver Springs, MD 20910. Phone: (800) 388-2227.

Conventional loan: A long-term loan a lender makes for the purchase of a home.

Convertible adjustable-rate mortgage: A mortgage, which starts as an adjustable-rate loan, but allows the borrower to convert the loan to affixed-rate mortgage during a specified period of time.

Conveyance: The transfer of title of property.

Conveyance tax: A tax imposed on the transfer of real property.

Co-signer: A second party who signs a promissory note and takes responsibility for the debt.

Cost-plus contract: A construction contract that determines the builder's profit based on a percentage of the cost of labor and materials.

Creative financing: Innovative home-financing arrangements that help sell a property.

Credit history: A record of an individual's current and past debt payments.

Creditor: An individual or institution to who a debt is owed.

Credit life insurance: Insurance that pays off a mortgage in the event of the borrower's death.

Credit rating: The degree of credit worthiness assigned to a person based on credit history and financial status.

Credit report: A credit bureau report that shows a loan applicant's history of payment made on previous debts. Several companies issue credit reports, but the three largest are trans Union Corp., Equifax and Experian (formerly TRW).

Credit repository: Large companies that gather financial and credit information from various sources about individuals who have applied for credit.

Debt service: The amount needed for payment of principal and interest on an amortized debt.

Debt service ratio: The relationship between the amounts of debt service to the net income. Most lenders will require a loan to have a ratio of every $1.00 of debt, to at least $1.25 dollars of net income or a ratio of 1 to 1.25.

Deed of trust: A document that transfers ownership of a piece of property.

Default: the failure to fulfill a duty or promise.

Delinquent mortgage: A mortgage that involves a borrower who is behind on payments. If the borrower cannot bring the payments up to date within a specified number of days, the lender may begin foreclosure proceedings.

Discounts points: Fees that a borrower pays at the time the lender makes the loan. A point equals 1 percent of the total loan amount.

Document needs list: A list of documents a lender requires when a potential submits a loan application. The required documents range from paycheck stubs to credit card statements.

Effective gross income: Additional income that a lender considers when assessing the loan application of a potential borrower.

End loan: The conversion from a construction loan to permanent financing a condominium buyer secures after all units in a project have been completed.

Fair Credit Billing Act: A federal law that governs credit and charge card billing errors, if a credit or charge card company violates any provision, consumers can sue to recover damages.

Fair Credit Reporting Act: A federal law passed in 1971 that regulates the activity of credit bureaus. It is designed to prevent inaccurate or obsolete information from staying in a consumer's credit file and requires credit bureaus to have reasonable procedures for gathering, maintaining and disseminating credit information. The act also requires credit bureaus to show a consumer their credit file if the consumer presents proper identification, although the bureau reserves the right to charge a fee for doing so.

Fair Debt Collection Practices Act: A federal law passed in 1977 that outlaws debtor harassment and other types of collection practices. The act regulates collection agencies, original creditors who set up a separate office to collect debts, and lawyers hired by the creditor to help collect overdue bills. An original creditor--the company or individual that originally granted the credit-is not covered by the act, but may be covered by similar measures approved by state governments.

Farmer's Home Administration: A U.S. Department of Agriculture agency that provides credit to farmers and rural residents.

Federal Home Loan Mortgage Corporation Law: The Federal Home Loan Mortgage Corporation, commonly known as Freddie Mac. The company buys mortgages from lending institutions, pools them with other loans and then sells shares to investors.

Fixed-rate mortgage: A home loan with an interest rate that will remain at a specific rate for the term of the loan. About 75 percent of all home mortgages have fixed rates.

Forbearance: A course of action a lender may pursue to delay foreclosure or legal action against a delinquent borrower.

Foreclosure: The legal process reserved by a lender to terminate the borrower's interest in a property after a loan has been defaulted. When the process is completed, the lender may sell the property and keep the proceeds to satisfy its mortgage and any legal costs. Any excess proceeds may be used to satisfy other liens or be returned to the borrower.

Forfeiture: The relinquishing of property rights by a delinquent borrower.

Fully amortized adjustable-rate mortgage: A mortgage that amortizes, or pays down, the balance of a loan.

Growing-equity mortgage: A fixed rate mortgage that increases payments over a specific period of time. The extra funds are applied to the principal.

Guarantee mortgage: A loan guaranteed by a third party, such as a government institution.

Good will: The definition of the intangible value of the business reputation of a specific business. The value is above fixtures, equipment and inventory.

Hazard insurance: This provision of landowners insurance covers damage by fire, wind or other disaster. All lenders require it before a loan is approved.

HUD-1 Uniform Settlement Statement: A closing statement or settlement sheet that outlines all closing costs on a real estate transaction or refinancing.

Index: Financial tables used by lenders to calculate interest rates on adjustable mortgages and on Treasury bills.

Initial interest rate: The original interest rate on an adjustable mortgage.

Insurable title: Title to property that a company agrees to insure against defects and disputes.

Insurance: Owners and buyers can purchase various types of insurance: hazard, private mortgage and earthquake. The policies guarantee compensation for specific losses.

Insurance binder: A temporary insurance arrangement usually put in force until a permanent policy can be obtained.

Interest: The fee borrowers pay to obtain a loan. It is calculated based on a percentage of the total loan.

Interest accrual rate: The rate at which interest accrues on a mortgage.

Interest only loan: This pays only the interest that accrues on the loan balance each month. Because each payment goes toward interest, the outstanding balance of the loan does not decline with each payment.

Interest rate: The sum, expressed as a percentage, charged for a loan. Interest payments on most home loans are tax-deductible.

Interest rate buy-down plans: For cash-short buyers, some sellers are willing to advance funds from the sale of the home to buy down the interest rate and reduce the buyer's monthly obligation.

Interest rate caps: A limit on the amount that can be charged to the monthly payment of an adjustable-rate mortgage during an adjustment period.

Interest rate ceiling: The highest interest a lender can charge for an adjustable-rate mortgage.

Investment property: Real estate that generates income, such as an apartment building or a rental house.

Judicial foreclosure: A procedure to handle foreclosure proceedings as civil matters.

Leasehold estate: An arrangement in which the borrower does not own a specific piece of property but possesses a long-term lease.

Liabilities: A borrower's debt and financial obligations.

Life cap: A limit on the amount that a loan rate can move during the term at the mortgage. For example, the rate on an adjustable-rate mortgage that begins at S percent and has a lifetime cap of 6 percentage points cannot rise above 11 percent, even if rates on fixed-rate mortgages soar to 20 percent.

Life cycle cost analysis: An analysis of a building projects expected operating, maintenance and replacement costs, calculated by an architect.

Loan application: The first step toward submitting a-commercial loan requires the borrower to itemize basic financial information.

Loan application fee: A fee charged by lenders to for making a loan application.

Loan commitment: A promise by a lender or other financial institution to make or insure a loan for a specified amount and on specific terms.

Loan origination fee: Most lenders charge borrowers an origination fee or points for processing a loan. A point is 1 percent of the total loan amount.

Loan processing fee: A fee charged by some lenders for gathering information to enable the lender to process the loan.

Loan term: The amount of a time set by the lender for a buyer to pay a mortgage. Most conventional loans have 30-year or 15-year terms.

Loan-to-value ratio: A technical measure used by lenders to assess the relationship of the loan amount to the value of the property.

Maximum financing: A loan amount within 5 percent of the highest loan-to-value ratio allowed for a property.

Merged credit report: A report that draws information from the Big Three credit-reporting companies: Equifax, Experian and TransUnion Corp.

Modification: A change in any of the terms of the loan agreement.

Mortgage: A legal document specifying a certain amount of money to purchase a home at a certain interest rate, and using the property as collateral.

Mortgagee: A bank or other financial institution that lends money to the borrower. The borrower is considered the mortgagor.

Mortgagor: The person who borrows money to purchase a house. The lender is called the mortgagee.

Mortgage acceleration clause: A clause, which allows a lender to demand that the entire balance of the loan, be repaid in a lump sum under certain circumstances. The acceleration clause is usually triggered if the home is sold, title to the property is changed, the loan is refinanced or the borrower defaults on a scheduled payment.

Mortgage banker: A company that provides home loans using its own money. The loans are usually sold to investors such as insurance companies and Fannie Mae.

Mortgage broker: A company that matches lenders with prospective borrowers who meet the lender's criteria. The mortgage broker does not make the loan, but receives payment from the lender for services.

Net cash flow: Investment property that generates income after expenses such as principal, interest, taxes and insurance are subtracted.

Net worth: The worth of a person or company based on the difference between total assets and liabilities.

No cash-out refinance: The amount of the new mortgage covers the remaining balance of the first loan, closing costs, any liens and cash no more than one (1) percent of the principal on the new loan.

Niche Lenders: Lenders who specialize in a certain narrow area of lending based on type of property, credit level or size of loans.

No-documentation loan: A loan application that does not require verification of income but typically is granted in cases of large down payments.

Non-recurring closing costs: Costs that are one-time only fees for such items as an appraisal, loan points, credit report, title insurance and a home inspection.

Note: The legal document that requires a borrower to repay a mortgage at a certain interest rate over a specified period of time.

Origination fee: A fee charged by most lenders--also called points--for processing a loan. A point is 1 percent of the total loan amount.

Owner financing: A transaction in which the seller of a property agrees to finance all or part of the purchase.

PITI (Principal, Interest, Taxes, and Insurance): When a buyer applies for a loan, the lender will calculate the principal, interest, taxes and insurance. The figure is designed to represent the borrower's actual monthly mortgage-related expenses.

Points: Fees charged by lenders at the time a loan is originated. A point is equal to 1 percent of the total loan.

Prepaid interest: Interest paid before it is due. For example, at the close of a real estate transaction borrowers usually pay for the interest on their loan that falls between the closing period and the first monthly payment.

Prepayment penalty: Lenders can impose a penalty on a borrower who pays a loan off before its expected end date.

Principle of progression: An appraisal term, which states that real estate of lower value, is enhanced by the proximity of higher-end properties.

Principle of regression: An appraisal term which states that the value of higher-end real estate can be brought down by the proximity of too many lower-end properties.

Property tax: Property taxes are calculated at about 1.5 percent of the current market value.

Property tax deduction: The U.S. tax code allows homeowners to deduct the amount they have paid in property taxes.

Property value: The value of a piece of property is based on the price a buyer will pay at a certain time.

Pro-ration: Agreed-upon percentages of certain expenses associated with a piece of property that must be paid by the buyer or the seller at the time of closing.

Purchase-money mortgage: A mortgage that a borrower obtains to acquire a property.

Quitclaim deed: A document that releases a party from any interest in a piece of real estate.

Rate-improvement mortgage: A loan with a clause that entitles a borrower to a one-time cut in the interest rate without going through refinancing.

Rate lock: When interest rates are volatile, many borrowers want to "lock in' an interest rate and many lenders will oblige, setting a limit on the amount of time the guaranteed interest rate Is in effect.

Real estate investment trusts (REIT): The trusts are publicly traded companies that own, develop and operate commercial properties.

Estate Settlement Procedures Act (RESPA): A federal law designed to make sellers and buyers aware of settlement fees and other transaction-related costs. RESPA also outlaws kickbacks in the real estate business.

Recording fee: A fee charged by real estate agents for conveying the sale of a piece of property into the public record.

Regulation Z: The federal code issued under the Truth-in-Lending Act, which requires that a borrower be advised in writing of all costs associated with the credit portion of a financial transaction.

Replacement reserve fund: Money that is set aside from the borrower's funds to replace property, such as a roof.

Restructured loan: A mortgage in which new terms are negotiated.

Second mortgage: Another loan placed upon a piece of property.

Secured loan: Any loan backed by collateral.

Security: A piece of property designated as collateral.

Settlement statement: A document that details who has paid what to whom.

Single purpose entity: A designated legal entity created for a special purpose like to hold a specific property to allow an owner or lender to have greater security from historical debt or liabilities.

Special deposit account: Rehabilitation mortgages require a special deposit account from which restoration and remodeling funds included in the loan are disbursed to the appropriate contractors as work is completed.

Standard payment calculation: A calculation that is used to determine the monthly payment necessary to repay the balance of a loan in equal installments.

Title: The actual legal document conferring ownership of a piece of real estate.

Title Company: Firms that ensure that the title to a piece of property is clear and provide title insurance.

Title insurance: A policy issued to lenders and buyers to protect any losses because of a dispute over the ownership of a piece of property.

Title risk: Possible impediments to the transfer of a title from one owner to another.

Treasury bills: Securities issued by the Treasury Department that have the full backing of the U.S. government.

Treasury index: An index used to determine interest rate changes for adjustable rate mortgages.

Two-step mortgage: An adjustable mortgage with two interest rates, one for the first five or seven years of the loan, and the other for the remainder of the loan term.

Variable interest rate: A loan rate that moves up and down based on factors including changes in the rate paid on bank certificates of deposit or Treasury bills.

Variable rate mortgage: A loan with an interest rate that hinges on factors such as the rate paid on bank certificates and Treasury bills.

Verification of deposit: Part of the loan process, in which a lender will ask a borrower's bank to sign a statement verifying the borrowers account balances and history.

Waiver: A voluntary relinquishing of certain rights or claims.

Warranty: A legally binding promise to do something in the future.

Wild deed: An improperly recorded deed.

Wraparound mortgage: A loan to a buyer for the remaining balance on a seller's first mortgage and an additional amount requested by the seller. Payments on both loans are made to the lender who holds the wraparound loan.

Printed in the USA
CPSIA information can be obtained
at www.ICGtesting.com
LVHW090846070924
790237LV00002B/143